D0592207

Buckeye

BUCKEYE

A Study of Coach Woody Hayes and
the Ohio State Football Machine

by Robert Vare

Harper's Magazine Press
Published in association with Harper & Row
New York

The transcript of the Woody Hayes interview that appears in Chapter 7 is reprinted by kind permission of WBNS TV, Columbus, Ohio.

Portions of this work originally appeared in *Sports Illustrated, Esquire, New Times,* and *Cleveland* magazine.

"Harper's" is the registered trademark of Harper & Row, Publishers, Inc.

BUCKEYE: COACH WOODY HAYES AND THE OHIO STATE FOOTBALL MACHINE. Copyright © 1974 by Robert Vare. All rights reserved. Printed in the United States of America. No part of this book may be used or reproduced in any manner whatsoever without written permission except in the case of brief quotations embodied in critical articles and reviews. For information address Harper & Row, Publishers, Inc., 10 East 53rd Street, New York, N.Y. 10022. Published simultaneously in Canada by Fitzhenry & Whiteside Limited, Toronto.

FIRST EDITION

ISBN: 0–06–129150–1

LIBRARY OF CONGRESS CATALOG CARD NUMBER: 74–3904

Acknowledgments

For their encouragement, advice and generosity, I thank James Toback, Benson Wolman, Kaye Kessler, Nancy Haberman, Jim Benagh, Ronald Shechtman, Charles Neighbors, Chuck Durfey, Tom Bendycki, Jack Torry and others who cannot be named. Special thanks go to Billy Salter, Clyde Haberman and Lee Eisenberg for their valuable editorial suggestions. The largest thanks of all belongs to my wife, Susan, without whom this book quite simply would never have materialized. And finally, my gratitude to Coach Hayes, for giving me what time he could and for being one of the most fascinating men in American life.

For Susan

Once there was a man who went to Heaven, where he was met by Saint Peter and taken to a gigantic football stadium for a game. Down on the field along the sidelines was a fat old man in a baseball cap, running back and forth, jumping up and down and gesturing hysterically.

"Who is that madman?" the new arrival asked Saint Peter.

"That's God," Saint Peter replied. "But he thinks he's Woody Hayes.

—An Ohio fable

Without winners there wouldn't even be any goddamned civilization.

The workday starts before dawn. About six o'clock you can see lights in the immaculate white house at 1711 Cardiff Road. The early beginning is a fact of life, even in the off-season. During the season, from the end of summer until the snow is on the ground, the house is still dark at daybreak: There just isn't time to sleep at home then.

It's May now. The schedule this time of year is less grinding. Still, there are reports to read, charts to study, statistics to digest, and they must be finished by breakfast time, *goddamnit.* A favorite maxim around the white house on Cardiff is: "Give me enough of a head start and I can beat Jesse Owens in a hundred-yard dash."

The house is a handsome, two-story frame structure with green shutters, built in the Forties—not much different from others in the neighborhood. Outside at the curb sits a white and brown Ranchero pickup, its sides encrusted with mud, its flatbed back carpeted in glowing green Astroturf. The vehicle is the butt of a few jokes around town. One has it that Coach Hayes holds scrimmages on the Astroturf while the pickup is moving. Whoever falls off gets cut from the squad.

It is apparent from the interior of the house that the same people have lived there for years. The modest furniture is in Early American style, well worn and comfortable. The shelves contain hundreds of books, many of them fat tomes on military history and international politics. Most of the books are about men of power: kings, princes, dictators, generals and presidents. But there are also volumes of fiction, plays and poetry. Few of the books are about football. Woody Hayes's explanation of this apparent oddity is that he already *knows* about football.

As well he should. He has been coaching a big-time college football team for twenty-three years. He has been coaching as long as or longer than any of the other legendary college coaches—Stagg of Chicago, Rockne of Notre Dame, Wilkinson of Oklahoma, Blaik of Army, Bryant of Alabama, Royal of Texas. And unless the family history of heart trouble finally overtakes him or somebody talks him into running for public office, he will be coaching the Ohio State Buckeyes for many years to come. Winners seldom retire.

With Woody Hayes prowling the sideline in his white short-sleeved shirt, a black baseball cap tugged down tight over his scalp, pounding his players on their helmets and

4

shoulder pads, growling at his assistant coaches, reviling referees, biting blood out from the heel of his hand in anger, devising battlefield strategy, keeping everybody on a tight leash, exercising total command, Ohio State and Columbus, Ohio, have become football landmarks. He has given the university and the city four national championships, nine Big Ten titles and four Rose Bowl victories. He wins three out of every four times he plays, and it's a good thing. In 1966, when his team had a losing season, people said he was getting old, and alumni donations to the school dropped by $500,-000. Winning is what football is all about, what Hayes believes America is all about. As he says, "Without winners there wouldn't even be any goddamned civilization."

By 6:45 breakfast is on the table. Hayes will, on a busy day, skip lunch and sometimes dinner, but never his breakfast of scrambled eggs, toast and three pieces of bacon.

During breakfast he pores over the morning newspaper, the Columbus *Citizen-Journal.* A member of the Scripps-Howard chain, the *Citizen-Journal* and its more conservative afternoon counterpart, the Columbus *Dispatch,* are steadfast voices of Midwestern Republicanism, doting on Boy Scout jamborees, patriotic celebrations and football. Every home-game Saturday in the fall, the *Dispatch* devotes its entire front page to the upcoming contest—complete with color photographs of Coach Hayes and his players, banner head-lines, line-ups of opposing teams, last-minute injury reports and details of anticipated strategies. The regular front-page news—the killings, bank robberies, and political scandals—gets shunted to the back page.

Woody Hayes's name appears in the hometown press al-most every day, with seldom a syllable of criticism. The local papers adore him and will do almost anything he asks. A few years ago, the *Dispatch* sports editor, a close friend, got the city desk to kill a story about a player who had been busted for possession of marijuana. Then the youngster was dropped from the team, quietly.

But in general, Hayes does not get along well with reporters, especially those who dwell on *bad news* and ask questions that are none of their business. Early in his career, before he learned how to handle the media, he told a writer from *Sports Illustrated* that he regularly lent money out of his own pocket to his needier players, some of whom paid him back. The revelation of his charity led to a Big Ten investigation and a one-year probation.

Now Hayes keeps almost all reporters *clear out to there.* Practice sessions are usually closed to all but the two local sportswriters who have covered him since he has been in Columbus, and who will continue to cover him as long as they can be trusted with family secrets. A writer who telephones an assistant coach or a player for a story will invariably be asked, "Does the old man know you're doing this?" They know that if something is leaked to the press, the talker will be hunted down and chastised. Family business is family business. *Hell,* if you have a fight with your wife, you sure don't want the neighbors to know about it.

The neighbors are beginning to get up now in the sturdy, well-kept houses of the exclusive Columbus suburb called Upper Arlington. It's a staid, affluent community, a mix of old-line and upwardly mobile WASPS holding high-paying positions in banks, insurance companies, brokerage firms and department stores. About a thousand of Upper Arlington's thirty thousand citizens teach at nearby Ohio State

University. Blacks don't live in Upper Arlington, except those employed as sleep-in domestics. Last year a black faculty member moved into town with his family and was awakened at 5:30 one morning by a shotgun blast through his living room.

There are few bars in Upper Arlington. The people drink at home or at one of the country clubs like the Scioto, where Jack Nicklaus, a local hero, learned to play golf.

The man at 1711 Cardiff is much more of a local hero. He guides central Ohio's most cherished institution. He leads its representative army. He runs its massive football machine. And the way he guides and leads and runs has brought to Columbus and Ohio State fame, pride and money. How many of these professors in Upper Arlington would even have their jobs, he asks, without the publicity he helped generate, the revenues he helped raise—simply by winning? Winners, he points out, get a good press, bring in big gate receipts, attract large alumni donations and earn fat television and radio contracts. Losers do not.

The doubters and detractors make him furious. At colleges across the country, a small but growing number of students, teachers, administrators, athletes and even coaches are raising questions about the role of big-time intercollegiate football in the American system of higher education. They say it is irrelevant, even corrupting, to the true goals of the university, and that it has become too costly, too political, too commercial, too professional and too exploitive in its pursuit of victory. To these critics, Woody Hayes is a symbol of what is wrong, presiding as he does over the model American college football machine—a vast conglomerate of money, high-pressure recruiting, tutoring and special treatment, out of which emerge winning teams. A football machine, these critics might argue, is like a political machine, its only goals power and self-preservation.

But to hell with the critics, says Hayes. To hell with the liberals who badmouth the game, the fault-finders who complain when he smashes a camera into a photographer's face or rips apart a sideline down marker. What have the critics ever done for football? Let the sonsofbitches whine about "*de*-humanization," about assaults on players for poor execution. Do they know that afterward he will go into the shower with those same players and soap down their backs?

By 7:15 the door of the white frame house swings open and a large, beefy man emerges, a clutch of papers and notebooks under his thick, muscular right arm. Several brisk steps later and Woody Hayes is behind the wheel of his pickup. As always, he turns the ignition key and pulls away from the curb without buckling the seat belt. A mind occupied with goal-line defenses, General Sherman's march through Georgia and Metternich's concept of the balance of power is too busy to remember seat belts.

The drive to work is not long. A couple of years ago Coach Hayes got on an ecology kick, sold his old car and walked to the office every day. Head cocked to one side, chest out, he marched around campus at a foot-soldier's clip. He enjoyed the pedestrian life. Grinning teenage girls would appear and hug him. "I just know my daddy would want me to do it," one told him. Up on High Street, the main campus drag, he held long discussions with students, particularly longhairs, whom he sought out and stopped Socratic-style with the question; "What is your main gripe against the university?" A lot of them didn't want to talk to him at first, but they did. The walking-talking custom ceased when he decided it was taking too much time from work.

From home, it's a little more than two miles to Hayes's office. Actually, he has two offices. One is on the second floor of St. John Arena, the home of the Ohio State athletic department. He has comfortable quarters there with high-backed armchairs, a large metal desk and a couple of secretaries to answer the phone and take messages on the few calls he might care to return. The walls are crowded with plaques and scrolls and pictures of generals—Westmoreland, Abrams, Walt—friends made on his four trips to Vietnam.

But he doesn't use that office much. The phones never stop ringing and there are too many people around. Most of the time he works alone at the North Facility, the football team's $1 million training center, a remote and quiet enclave in the agricultural section of campus—far away from prying eyes.

The pickup turns right onto Lane Avenue and the many red-brick buildings of Ohio State come into view. It is one of the largest universities in the country, with an enrollment of more than 45,000 students, a land area of 3,500 acres and an endowment of $43 million. Glancing to the right, along the banks of the Olentangy River, Hayes can see the new $4.6 million Drake Student Union, a stately cast-concrete structure with a theater and marina. To the left is the $6.5 million Fawcett Center for Tomorrow, a tower of dark red brick, where conferences are held and alumni and friends of the university can get a spotless, hermetically sealed room to sleep in. Coach Hayes puts up high school recruits there overnight, then takes them to breakfast in the dining room while he impresses upon them the wisdom of attending Ohio State.

Everywhere he looks as he drives, gleaming new buildings

are up or going up. He likes to boast about how beautiful the campus is—a lot better looking than some of the students, that's for damned sure. None of these fine modern buildings was there before he came. He believes his hard work helped put them there, his *winning*.

If the pickup continued east along Lane Avenue, then turned south on Neil Avenue, it would come to the campus gates where, in the spring of 1970, angry students blocked off traffic to protest university policies. The demonstration, combined with bombing raids in Cambodia and student killings at Kent State University one hundred and thirty-five miles away, touched off a wave of disorders that eventually shut down the school for ten days. Characteristically, Hayes waded into the thick of the disturbances and made impassioned speeches. But he used words like *loyalty, opportunity* and *goals*—the kind of words he uses with his players—and many of the students booed, heckled and laughed at him. Later, he offered a different version of what happened, and took some credit for quelling the uprising.

The pickup pulls into the North Facility parking lot. His is usually the first car to arrive and always the last to leave. He throws open the steel door of the building and enters at full stride, walking quickly down the long corridor into an equipment room. A moment later he is joined by a frail man who moves slowly and carries a stack of towels. His name is Phil, and for close to three decades he has been the equipment repairman for the Ohio State football team, creating braces and harnesses so that players with cracked ribs and shoulder separations will not miss games. Among other things, Phil polishes his boss's shoes to a high military shine.

Coach Hayes rushes over and shakes Phil's hand while clasping him by the shoulder. Even though he sees Phil nearly every day, Hayes will take the time now to sit down and talk with him over a cup of coffee, because he values loyal people. Phil's health is not good—last year part of his larynx was removed because it was cancerous. And now his daughter is in the hospital for an operation. Before the conversation is over, Hayes promises to visit her, a pledge he will keep. He is a congenital hospital visitor, spending more time with the sick and infirm than some doctors. Hospital visits, along with weddings and funerals, are the staples of his social life.

He continues down the hall to Room 147. There is no name on the door but everyone knows it's where to find "Coach." He's also called "The Old Man," "The Boss," "Woody," and "Ol' Woody," but never "Good Ol' Woody." At least not to his face. He loathes the idea that anybody might think he, Wayne Woodrow Hayes, is mellowing.

The office, a tiny, windowless room in subdued shades of tan and yellow, recalls a monk's cell. In the corner is a hard-cushioned, red-vinyl couch where he sleeps at night during the season. He likes to be near films and charts and scouting reports should inspiration arrive at 4 A.M. There is also a blackboard for diagramming plays, a chair, a desk and a telephone, its number known to only a few. That's the telephone on which President Nixon called several years ago to ask Hayes to head the Peace Corps.

It is not yet 7:30 but already his assistant coaches are waiting for him around the corridor outside Room 151, a large classroom with a film projector and a seven-foot-high chart detailing the success of every Ohio State offensive play the previous season. The nine full-time assistants are always on time or early, because Hayes considers tardiness unpardonable, like fumbling inside the twenty-yard line or knocking the military. The assistants are almost all young, talented, hard-working and ambitious. He hires them for these attributes—as well as for obedience. When he scowls they scowl; when he laughs they laugh. There are few men who command loyalty to the extent Woody Hayes does and few who preach it so relentlessly.

The daily meeting starts as soon as Hayes enters the room. He sits in a swivel chair behind a big desk in front of a blackboard, while the assistants occupy smaller desk-chairs in the first two rows. His desk is usually cluttered with papers. While not an especially orderly man, Coach Hayes is a meticulous planner.

As the first order of business he is given a complete list of all players who failed to attend yesterday afternoon's workout. It doesn't matter that the practice was "voluntary," it being late spring and close to final exams. Every transgressing player's name is recorded, even that of the lowliest freshman who will probably never get into a game. Nobody misses a day in the gym without Coach Hayes's knowing about it. He has to keep track of every one of his hundred and fifteen players, because they are not just athletes; they are pieces of the Machine.

He studies the list, his eyes stopping at one name.

"Rocco didn't show up?" he asks.

"No, he didn't, Coach," replies George Hill, the defensive coordinator, accountable for every player on the defense. Hill, in his late thirties, is Hayes's chief assistant. He is next in the line of succession, but still a long way from the throne.

The player they're talking about is Rocco Rich, a linebacker from Canton, Ohio. When Rich entered Ohio State he was such a ferocious tackler that people admiringly nicknamed him the "Canton Pig." But because of bad knees Rich has spent almost as many hours on the operating table as on the field. Now at the end of his junior year, he is so discouraged about his career, he doesn't even show up at the gym.

HAYES: Now goddamnit, what the hell is wrong with him?

HILL: He came to see me the other day, Coach. Said the doctor told him to take it easy until the fall.

HAYES: Oh, shit! Now that's just a lot of crap! No sir! I don't believe that shit for a minute! How're his grades?

HILL: They're down there, Coach. I don't know if he's gonna pass that chemistry course, and—

HAYES: Jeezus Ch-rist! We've really got ourselves a winner, don't we? He's getting married, too, isn't he? I got the goddamn invitation the other day.

HILL: I was just about to tell you about that, sir. I think it's on the twenty-second of next month.

HAYES: Shoot! Shoot! Shoot! He isn't gonna be worth a fart next year, is he? As if he didn't have enough problems, goddamnit. Y'know it really takes the edge off a football player when there's a warm little ass next to him in the bed! I know it's true because I've done some research on it.

The assistants rarely challenge him. If they hang on his every word, they have good reason. He once spent a staff meeting reading and lecturing on *Quotations from Chairman Mao,* then gave them a written exam on the material. It wasn't that he suddenly wanted to turn his coaches into Maoists. He just wanted to see how well they were listening.

The assistants are accustomed to Hayes's fits of temper and can tell how angry he is from the interjections he uses. He's only a little angry when he says, "Shoot! Shoot! Shoot!" He's angrier when he says "goddamnit" or "Jeezus Ch-rist" or "sonofabitch" or "sonofagoddamnbitch." He's angrier still when he says "goddamnit to hell" or "fuck." If the blood is really roiled, he'll break into a rambling, sputtering diatribe, waving arms and banging fists. Then he will begin to lisp—an imperfection he has had since childhood—and the words will come out *thonofabitch . . . Jeethuth Ch-ritht!* At the top of his rage, he will throw something, a chair, a desk, a film projector. Once an assistant had to inform him that a talented quarterback from northern Ohio whom they were courting had decided to go to the University of Michigan, the hated archrival "team up north" as he calls it. Hearing the news, Hayes picked up a projector and hurled it a good thirty-five feet across the meeting room. There's nothing worse than losing a good Ohio boy to Michigan.

The only thing that might be worse is not knowing what he has to know. He must know who missed yesterday's practice and anything else that might conceivably be at cross-purposes with winning. If a player does poorly on a test, the coach must know it. If a player is living with a woman, the coach must know it. If a player takes part in a demonstration, the coach must know it. And if a player hangs out with people who smoke pot or eat no meat or wear green underwear, the coach must know that, too.

Usually he can find somebody who will tell him. His intelligence network is formidable. All over campus and town, there are reliable eyes and ears. Several times he has dropped youngsters for offending his moral code. But the truth is, they also weren't very good football players.

Discussion in the meeting room continues. There are important questions to be answered: "How's his knee? . . . What's his weight? . . . Where's he going to be this summer? . . . Why is he moving out of the dorm? . . . Is he running every day? . . . What courses is he taking? . . . How're his grades? . . . Is he passing everything?"

His preoccupation with the academic status of his players goes beyond the ordinary coachly concern for eligibility. The son of a school superintendent, Hayes holds not only a bachelor's degree in English and history, but also a master's degree in educational administration, and he views himself as an educator. The day before an away game he has been known to drag his team and coaches to a lecture on the opponent's campus. He loves to brag about how many of his players get their diplomas. Let the liberals talk about football factories and jocks. Why, he can teach a boy more in two months than some of those professors do in four years. *His* players graduate. He keeps after them until they do, even if it is two, three, five years after they have closed out their Buckeye football careers. If they continue to procrastinate, he may telephone them early in the morning: "Now goddamn-it, when are you gonna get that goddamn sheepskin?"

John Brockington, formerly of Ohio State and now a Green Bay Packer, is paid more than one hundred thousand dollars a year for being one of the best runners in pro football. And every time John Brockington comes back to Room 147 he is greeted warmly with the words, "Now goddamnit, Brock, when are you going to get that goddamn sheepskin?"

The sheepskin is everything, or at least it's Hayes's answer to the doubters who talk about exploitation in college football. As always, his interest is in end results. If you have that sheepskin, how the hell can anybody say you didn't get an education?

The coaches' meeting lasts well into the morning. For lunch Hayes usually sends out to McDonald's, or, if he feels like going out, he may dart over to the sandwich counter at the Big Bear, a supermarket on Lane Avenue.

If time permits, he goes to his favorite restaurant in Columbus, the Jai Lai [sic]. The Jai Lai is all pink and done up in an architectural style that can be described only as neo-Moorish-rococo, a piece of kitsch Casablanca set down in the heart of Middle America. Inside, under the watchful eye of a maitre d' who looks like George Raft, veteran waitresses serve steak and potatoes and other equally exotic American dishes. The Jai Lai's highlight, however, is the life-sized, black-and-white photograph hanging on the right as you come in. It's a picture of Woody Hayes in full battlefield dress. He's wearing the baseball cap with the letter O above the peak, an Ohio State sweatshirt and a whistle on a cord around his thick neck. His face is locked in a frown. The inscription on the photograph—TO THE JAI LAI: IN ALL THE WORLD THERE'S ONLY ONE—suits the subject as well as the surroundings.

Downtown there are restaurants that serve European cuisine and attract a fancier clientele. They would love to have Woody Hayes as a customer, because if you run a business in Columbus, it is no small matter to have your name linked with his. But Hayes won't go to those places. Food doesn't have to be *that* good, he says, and besides, he doesn't want people to think he's gone high-hat. A few years ago, when a promotionally minded Cadillac dealer offered him a free car, he turned it down, saying "I'm not the Cadillac type." Would Darrell Royal, Ara Parseghian or Bear Bryant have so demurred?

Hayes is not a man who goes in for flash or frills. Off the football field he wears shapeless double-knit blazers and trousers. His shirt is usually short sleeved, white or pale blue, his ties broadly striped. Long-sleeved shirts and expensive, stylish clothes are for playboys.

He is childlike in his handling of money matters. He owns no credit cards and sometimes finds himself caught short in restaurants and gas stations. His coaching salary is twenty-nine thousand four hundred dollars a year, an astonishingly low figure in light of his seniority and success. Three times when his employers moved to correct the injustice by paying him more, he refused, explaining that he was simply doing his bit for the university and inflation. He has no desire whatever for personal wealth, a trait not usually associated with registered Republicans.

At lunch Hayes might be accompanied by someone like Jim Roseboro, the Columbus-born black man who ran in the Buckeye backfield with Hopalong Cassady twenty years ago. He likes Roseboro, whose brother John was for many years a Major League catcher. A couple of years ago Hayes suggested to some political people in town that it might be nice to have a black ex–Ohio State football player on the City Council, even if that person were a Democrat and, worse, had fumbled three times in a Michigan game. If only Councilman Jim Roseboro had gotten his law degree, he, Hayes, might now be able to push him for something higher, like Mayor of Columbus or Governor of Ohio.

Coach Hayes's endorsement is one of the most sought-after political prizes in the state. In 1960, when a group of students asked him to greet vice presidential candidate Lyndon Johnson during a campaign stop on campus, he declined, solemnly explaining that the coach of the Ohio State football team ought to be above partisan politics. A month

17

later, when Richard Nixon addressed a large rally at the State Capitol downtown, there at his side was Wayne Woodrow Hayes.

He himself has had lots of feelers over the years from political pros. All things considered, how could he miss—particularly if the election took place after an undefeated season? But he probably won't ever throw his baseball cap into the political arena. Candidates have to do and say too many things they don't want to do and say. Besides, he already holds one of the highest offices in the state.

Lunch is over and well before two o'clock Hayes is back in the meeting room. Usually this is the time he sifts through the dozens of letters he receives every day from all over the country.

Dear Mr. Hayes:
Having been a fan of yours for quite a few years, I am taking the liberty to advise you about a youngster that might be of interest to you . . .
                            Sincerely,
                            R.L. Toledo, Ohio

Dear Sir:
Do you know of someone who might be interested in an assistant varsity football coaching position?
As of today we have a vacancy . . .
                            Sincerely,
                            T.M.B. Spokane, Washington

Dear Fathead:
You ought to retire from football as soon as possible. You are the worst coach in the country, bar none. You couldn't lead a girl

scout troop to victory. I hope you quit now so I won't have to watch your ugly dumb fat face on television next year.

Unsigned. Cleveland, Ohio

On an average afternoon in the off-season, there will be plenty of visitors to see Coach Hayes. Many of them come as supplicants. They want loans, recommendations for jobs, help in getting into graduate school, a chance to do some business with the university, to get some teacher off their backs, to return to his good graces, a break. Hayes bends over backward to say yes, and he usually lets them know what he can do right away. Unless the person is someone he feels has betrayed him. Then he can be pitiless.

Just how pitiless was discovered by Ross Moore, one of the finest high school quarterbacks ever to come out of Pennsylvania. Everyone agreed Moore would some day be Ohio State's quarterback. But early in his freshman year, he came up limping in practice from a vicious gang-tackle, his knee shattered and his season finished. After an operation, Moore came back the next season, only to sustain another injury, this time to his shoulder. Now Coach Hayes was furious, convinced his young quarterback was malingering. He decided to punish Moore, working him against the first-team defense in practice, where he took a pounding every day, but never using him in games. By the summer before his senior year, Moore got fed up and quit. But ending Moore's athletic ambitions wasn't enough. He had to teach Moore nobody was going to defy him and get away with it. Moore's scholarship was taken away. Other players whose scholarships had been cut had meekly backed off and kept quiet. But Moore, a brash, rebellious type, hired a lawyer, and at a university hearing won his back.

19

Yet for every player Hayes sets out to break, there are dozens who get his helping hand. In general it pays to do favors. Years ago he arranged for the athletic department to pick up the hospital bill for a player named Lou Fischer, who had been badly injured in a fall off a diving board. Fischer had undergone surgery and had been forced to stay in the hospital several months. When he left he was handed a bill for six thousand dollars, a sum he couldn't pay. In 1970 Fischer, by then a millionaire fast-food tycoon in Baltimore, donated four hundred thousand dollars to Ohio State so that artificial turf could carpet the stadium football field. Twenty years later and Fischer had not forgotten.

The afternoon work goes on at full speed. The administrators arrive with information about athletic department contributions. Someone is always giving money. Coach Hayes must know who is giving what and when, to find out how well his wheedling, cajoling and arm-twisting is working.

"John gave a thousand?" he asks.

"That's right, Coach," comes the reply.

"Gee, that's just great! I knew he'd come around. And Harry gave five thousand. Great! Great! I had to go out to his house to see him. Y'know he won't give a penny unless I go out there myself."

The trainers come with injury reports. The academic counselor or "brain coach" drops by to brief him on the scholastic progress of his freshmen. At 5:30 Woody Hayes is still pouring it on. As the years pass and the hair turns whiter, the workdays get longer, the days-off fewer. Several summers ago Hayes cut short his first trip to Europe, a tour of the Swiss Alps, after telephoning his office and learning that one of his starters was on the verge of flunking out. He naps more often than he used to, but friends say he works harder now, at the age of sixty-one, than ever before.

Next on the Hayes agenda may be a dinner of civic officials, a booster club, a professional group or an organization such as the Elks, Kiwanis or Rotarians. As a speaker, he is in heavy demand around the state. There is never a set speech, yet the format rarely varies. He always leads off with a couple of jokes. "Did you hear the one about the guy at the nudist camp with a beard? . . . Somebody had to go to the grocery." No matter how awful the joke, it's greeted by deafening laughter. The bulk of the speech abounds with chamber of commerce talk, confidence in the team, high hopes for the university and affirmations of football's lofty purpose—all of the above spiked with antiliberal calumnies. After the speech even the most prominent politicians and businessmen will seek him out. Tomorrow they can tell their clients, associates and friends: "I was talking to Woody last night . . ."

Often the banquets are several hours from Columbus. On the trip back, he may pull over to the side of the road, climb into the back of the pickup and stretch out on the Astroturf. Woody Hayes sleeps like a baby on Astroturf.

On nights when there are no speaking engagements, he will drive over to the Ohio State Faculty Club, where a place is set for him at a large round table of venerable professors. Regardless of the subject at dinner, whether it is an event in the news, Herodotus, the American Revolution, Shakespeare or Walt Disney, he is certain to dominate the conversation. "Never ask Woody Hayes for the time," a rival coach once said, "unless you want to find out how a watch is made." Hayes fancies himself a student of history, especially military history, and even the old academics stand in awe of his amazing recall of detail. The waitresses, most of them Ohio State students, serve him quickly. They know his habits and are always ready for the question: "Now tell me, young lady, what is your major gripe against the university?"

After dinner, he may stop back over at the North Facility to study game films. In the course of a year, someone once said, Coach Hayes sees more reels of film than Darryl F. Zanuck, viewing and reviewing every possible detail of his team's or an opponent's game. One snowy Saturday night in February, a friend telephoned him at the meeting room and was not surprised when he answered the phone. "I'm watching the films of the Ohio U.–Bowling Green game," Hayes said. "You ought to come up and see 'em. It's a helluva game."

The hour is late when the pickup heads home. Most of Hayes's Upper Arlington neighbors are already in bed, having spent the evening at home watching TV or playing bridge. His wife, Anne, is accustomed to his routine and will probably not wait up for him. She herself is a popular after-dinner speaker, making a couple of appearances a week.

The pickup swings past the massive Ohio Stadium where Hayes's beloved Buckeyes play. It's a dinosaur: gray, triple-decked and horseshoe-shaped, with a capacity of eighty-seven thousand. University trustees had the foresight to build it in 1922 when Coach Hayes was only nine years old. Now they need every inch of space to pack in the people. For twenty-one of Hayes's twenty-three years coaching in that stadium, Ohio State has led every school in the country in home attendance. *What the hell happened those two years anyway?* He should do some research on that. Demand a recount.

Let the goddamned doubters snivel about winning at any cost. Winning was what brought in those eighty-seven thousand people, was good for the people, good for the university, good for the city, good for the state and, when you come right down to it, good for *the whole goddamned country. Hell,* they could fill *two hundred fifty thousand* seats for a game if they had them. Some day the university might build a giant superstadium, the biggest in America, and name it after him. They could cover it with a gigantic plastic baseball cap and call it the "Woodydome." You know, it wouldn't be a bad idea. Tomorrow he just might call the president of the university and run it up the flagpole.

It's after midnight when the pickup turns onto tree-lined Cardiff Road. Regardless of how tired he is, he always reads for an hour before going to bed. What'll it be tonight? Maybe that new book on Lincoln. Perhaps some Maupassant, or a little Santayana.

Tomorrow the schedule is going to be even tougher. He's committed to speak at a clinic up in Akron for some junior-high-school football players. A good strong influence is exactly what some of these young kids today need. There are so many people to talk to, films to see, reports to study, books to read, speeches to deliver, meetings to conduct, preparations to make. Tomorrow he'll have to get up even earlier, drive himself even harder, if he's going to get all his work done, if he's going to beat Jesse Owens in a hundred-yard dash.

23

2

We're tearing down all our heroes in America!

"Will he have time to talk to me today?"

The voice on the other end of the phone belonged to Woody Hayes's secretary. It was tentative, ill at ease.

"I don't see too much here on the schedule this afternoon," she said. "He's got the Dayton lawyers tonight and . . . let's see . . . nothing for tomorrow except the Portsmouth Rotarians. . . . I haven't seen him yet today, though. . . . Would you like me to have him call you and maybe make an appointment?"

Before arriving in the spring of 1973, I had been warned about seeking a formal audience, about the unrelieved misery other writers had encountered. Reports almost unanimously described Hayes as abrasive, single-minded, petulant and bitterly anti-press. In recent months there had been a famous attack on a Los Angeles *Times* photographer before the Rose Bowl game, and rumors of a blow struck against another photographer and a foiled attempt on a newspaper reporter.

"He's an unpredictable sonofabitch," said a friend who, while on assignment for *Look* magazine, had suffered a humiliating ejection after having scheduled an interview two months in advance. "The best thing to do is just drop in unannounced. He'll probably throw you out. But there's a chance he'll feel like haranguing you for an hour or two."

Another writer familiar with the manners and mores of the coach had urged that I get a haircut, shave my beard, wear a jacket and tie, give a firm handshake and proclaim my love for Hayes's hero, General George Patton.

"This is a pretty light week," the secretary said. "Spring practice ended last Saturday, and he probably won't be bothered by many people today. He doesn't usually tell me where he is but I guess he's over at the North Facility."

When it was built in 1970, the North Facility was officially named the Ernie Biggs Athletic Training Facility after a trainer who had ministered to Ohio State athletes for thirty years. Well removed from the bustle of campus, the building stands down the road from the Department of Poultry Science at the edge of rolling pastureland. It's an austere, cinder-block and aluminum fortress with a surrounding five-foot-high cyclone fence, cross-bar gates, heavy doors, metal burglar-alarm tape on the windows and other grim reminders that strangers are not welcome. The stark military bearing is at odds with the grazing cows and frolicking ponies nearby. It's as if a giant Quonset hut had been set down in

25

the middle of a Grandma Moses painting.

It was close to noon when I jerked open the front door and walked down a long, empty, gray-tiled corridor, passing several rooms with universal gyms, whirlpool baths and assorted technology of football. Near the end of the hall at Room 147, my knock produced no answer, and hearing nothing inside, I turned to leave. Ten retracing steps down the corridor, I heard the sound of the door being thrown open. There, standing in the doorway, was a hulking man, his large arms folded above a stomach that protruded like a glacial boulder. He was wearing a scarlet windbreaker and baggy gray pants, the colors of an Ohio State loyalist. He had neatly trimmed, ash-white hair that was combed straight back and a neck thick enough to support a Rodin head. The small, hazel eyes flashed cold fire, the thin lips curled in a bellicose scowl. There was no doubt that I was in the uniquely disquieting presence of Wayne Woodrow Hayes, the terrible-tempered dragon of the gridiron, molder of great football teams, smiter of players and press, sacker of down markers, student of history, military strategist, brooder, brawler, high priest of Middle America.

"How did you find me?" he asked softly, as if anything more than a whisper might activate his personal volcano.

"Your secretary told me that from the looks of your schedule, you'd probably be over here."

He winced as he might if one of his offensive tackles had jumped offsides. His lips were closed tight as a coffin.

"Nope," he said slowly, each word consuming a full beat, "I probably won't fire her for this. But I'll tell you this: I'm gonna give her *some kind of hell.* I'm gonna chew her butt out."

"But she really isn't the one to blame—"

26

"Now goddamnit. She knows she's not supposed to give out my schedule, *particularly to fellas like you.* Now I'm gonna have to straighten her out. I've already decided I'm not gonna fire her, but she needs to be straightened out. That's all. I'll do it sometime when nobody's around because I don't want people to hear her crying. She's a crier."

Hayes leaned over and took a long drink from a water fountain. He wiped the corners of his mouth with the back of his enormous hand.

"Y' know," he snorted, "you fellas from the press are not exactly my favorite people."

"So I've been told," I said. "But I wouldn't want you to pigeonhole me as a typical member of the press any more than you would want me to regard you as a typical football coach."

For an instant the tautness in Hayes's face disappeared, but only for an instant. He checked himself.

"Aw, shit! I know some people think I'm just a *big dumb football coach.* Maybe I'm *not* all that smart. But y' know, I have a saying: I may not be able to outsmart too many people, but I *can* outwork 'em. Yessir, I can *sure outwork* 'em." He squinted up his eyes to emphasize the point. "Anyway, to get back to your little thing here . . . I'm just gonna have to say I don't want to get involved. First of all I just don't have time. I'm much too busy to sit down and shoot the shit with a fella like you. Y' see, another thing is I've just been burned so goddamn many times. Every time I've talked to a writer I've regretted it, because you fellas end up *twisting* everything.

"Now take last year's Rose Bowl game. We go out there and lose to a fine USC team. So what do the goddamned people out there write about? They don't write about the wonderful football team which they had out there. They write about nothing but Woody Hayes beating up on a photographer. I get on the plane out there to go home and the reporters send me a message: 'Won't you come out and give us a statement?' I send 'em a message back that they don't need any help from me to tear down the game of football. They knew what they were gonna write without hearing what I had to say. So why even bother to talk to me? Y' see, this embitters a fella. I get so goddamn mad every time I think about it I want to put my foot through a goddamned window."

His voice was growing more strident. Now he was waving an index finger in front of my nose.

"I know just how Nixon feels. You fellas are out to destroy him. Just like a bunch of goddamned vultures. Aw, it's no secret. That's why this thing is all over the goddamn front page. You've been out to get Nixon for more than twenty years.

"Y' know, it's a funny thing," he went on in milder tones, "but the press—fellas like that *me*-golomaniac Jack Anderson—kept mighty quiet when Nixon had an election stolen from *him* in 1960. No, sir, there wasn't anything on the front page then about how Daley over there in Illinois came up with all those votes from people who weren't registered. Y' know that if Kennedy hadn't won Illinois, Dick Nixon would have been President back there in 1960. Not too many people know this, but Kennedy offered Dick Nixon the Presidency, and Dick Nixon turned him down because he thought it would tarnish the office to be forfeited like that. Now I've done some research on that and I know it's true."

28

Hayes took another drink from the fountain. The break provided a chance to edge a word in.

"I understand you're a good personal friend of the President."

"Well, we're pretty good friends, I guess. I met him back in '57, I think it was, after we had upset Iowa. He was Vice-President then and we were over at Senator Bricker's house having dinner. I remember he asked me an awful lot of questions about the game and football in general, and I asked him a lot of questions about foreign policy. I'll tell you this much: Back then he knew a helluva lot more about football than he did about foreign policy.

"But Nixon seems to have learned a lot since then, and I think history is gonna regard him as one of our greatest Presidents, one of our greatest *statesmen.* You just don't know how important it was to get together with Russia and China. It was one of the greatest achievements in the history of the world. And now this Watergate thing comes up and all of a sudden we've got a President who's got to go and negotiate with the other world powers from *weakness.* Now this is one thing you learn never to do. This is a *disaster* for America. It makes us the laughing stock of the whole goddamned world.

"Y' see, when people start laughing at you that's when you're really in trouble, boy. They tell me that goddamn show *Laugh-In* went off the air because they just plain ran out of people to make fun of. To me, there's nothing worse than being laughed at. Why, I'd much rather be spit on than laughed at. You're goddamned right I would. So you see why it makes me bitter when I see this Watergate inflated all out of proportion by you fellas. I'm a student of history and I've

29

been just sick as hell at what's happening in this country. You can see the pattern just as clear as day. We're tearing down all our heroes in America! There's just no respect anymore for anything, goddamnit. Now you take your sports or your military or your politics. They've gotten to and destroyed just about every sports figure and general we've ever had. Or take your Presidency. They've torn apart every single one, even George Washington. About the only one left is Abraham Lincoln and he was without any doubt the greatest man who ever lived. I call him the ultimate winner. It wouldn't surprise me one bit if they got to Lincoln too before too long."

The eyes were burning now with messianic intensity. Suddenly the voice dropped and became a whisper again. He leaned forward so that his face, for the moment mournful, was only inches away.

"Now I've done some research on this, and I can tell you something that's so true it isn't even funny. A society that's always tearing down its heroes is a *suicidal* society. A civilization without heroes isn't going to *be* a civilization much longer. I'll be a sonofabitch if I'm not right as hell on that."

Just then a tall, muscular young man stepped out from one of the equipment rooms. He was favoring his right leg. Woody Hayes noticed him right away and waved.

"Hello, Kurt," he bellowed, his face brightening. "How's it going?"

The young man's name was Kurt Schumacher. A junior, 6' 4", 248 pounds, Schumacher was a certain starter next season at offensive tackle. He was limping because he had twisted his left ankle a few weeks before, during spring practice.

"How's that ankle coming?" Hayes inquired.

"O.K., Coach," said Schumacher in flat Midwestern tones.

"Are you doing those exercises for it?"

"Which ones do you mean, Coach?"

"Now I'm talking about getting up on your toes and dropping back down again, son," said Hayes, giving a demonstration in which he extended his arms to the side and rocked back and forth on the balls of his feet. "That's the best way to strengthen these ankles."

"Oh, yeah," said Schumacher. "I'm at the point where I can do about ten of those, sir."

"Ten, huh?" said Hayes. "Well, gee, that's just great. That is really just great as hell."

"The only thing is, I'm still not really walking right yet."

"Aw, don't worry about that, son. You just keep getting up on those toes and you'll be walking good as new. Every day do a few more than you did the previous day."

"Yes, sir."

"Now how're your grades, Kurt?"

"Oh, they're O.K., Coach."

"Are you passing everything?" Hayes persisted.

"Oh, definitely. No problem at all."

"Great! Great! Great! Now you're *not* gonna get complacent and forget to study for finals, are you?"

Schumacher grinned. "I've already started studying, Coach."

"All right now, you keep it up. Keep up the hard work. Hey, by the way, I hear you're getting married next month."

"Yes, Coach." Schumacher nodded. "Early next month."

Woody Hayes watched his young lineman move with mincing steps down the hall until he was out of earshot. "Helluva kid. Aw, he's just a dandy kid." Hayes beamed, revealing a set of tiny, square teeth, gapped in front. "Y' see, his parents died when he was quite a young boy and an aunt had to raise him. I guess he must be pretty lonesome now, so he's gonna get married. It's not gonna help his football any, but I pretty well understand why he's doing it."

Schumacher had just about made it to the front door when Hayes called out, "Don't slack off on those exercises now, Kurt. Always remember to do more tomorrow than you have done today!"

This last instruction seemed to be addressed less to Schumacher than to me. At that moment, Coach Hayes was looking me straight in the eye, saying, "That's something *you* should always remember—do more tomorrow than you have done today."

He let the words sink in. "Do you know who said that? Well, sir, that's Emerson—Ralph Waldo Emerson. He said it in his essay on 'Compensation.' Have you ever read that?"

"A long time ago."

"Isn't it one of the greatest goddamned things ever written? Y' see, Thoreau was a cop-out. He spent the last thirty years of his life in seclusion because he didn't want to live in the world of men. That to me is a cop-out. Even when he went to jail it was only for a night and his aunt bailed him out the next morning. Now Emerson was a *doer*. He could talk to people on all levels. He could talk to the Phi Beta Kappa Society one day and to a bunch of farmers the next. He was a man of action who believed in working within the system."

Woody Hayes looked at his watch. For forty-five minutes he had been rooted to the same spot. "All right now, let's go into the office and sit down. Maybe we can answer some of your questions."

The office was a small, windowless room with a tiny desk piled high with papers, a couple of folding chairs and dozens of books. I scanned some of the titles: *Profiles in Courage, Portraits of Power, The Story of the FBI, Six Crises, The Anatomy of Revolution, Jonathan Livingston Seagull.* There were also biographies of generals—Patton, Rommel, Eisenhower, Sherman, MacArthur—and anthologies—*Great Speeches of the World, Famous People of the World*—and two shelves of Time-Life capsule books.

Woody Hayes motioned me to sit down. He put on a pair of silver-rimmed glasses that made him look like a meaty old barn owl. Then he picked up a worn, dog-eared paperback from the top of a stack of books and began flipping through its pages, some of which had been heavily underlined in black felt-tipped pen. Hayes unzipped his windbreaker, took a seat on the other side of the office and stretched out his legs.

"All right now, listen to this man Emerson," he commanded. "Now this is from your essay on 'Compensation.' Listen to this and maybe you'll learn something."

As he started to read, the voice was soft and loving, the cadence slow and even, like a minister rendering scripture at a Sunday service.

"For every strength there is a consequent weakness. Every excess causes a defect; every defect an excess. Every sweet hath its sour; every evil its good. For everything you have missed, you have gained something else. And for everything you gain, you lose something."

Hayes looked up. "Emerson's just right as hell on that," he said. "Now the greatest player I ever had playing for me was Hop Cassady, and Hop Cassady was also about the *smallest* who ever played for me. He was just a little guy. Only weighed about a hundred fifty-five pounds soaking wet. And he wasn't too fast either. But he *compensated.* He compensated for that lack of size and speed. First, he was just about the guttiest little guy I ever saw. Second, he was a goddamn *smart* football player. There was nobody could follow blockers better than old Hop."

The memory of his beloved charge brought a little moisture to the eyes of Woody Hayes. He turned a page, like someone leafing through an album of nostalgic snapshots, and found another passage.

"Say now, this'll really shake you up," he promised.

"The President has paid dear for his White House. It has commonly cost him all his peace, and the best of his manly attributes. To preserve for a short time so conspicuous an appearance before the world he is content to eat dust before the real masses who stand erect behind the throne."

"Now the amazing thing about that," Hayes said, "is that it was written more than a hundred years ago. Now just tell me one goddamned thing. Is that relevant to what's happening today with this Watergate thing or isn't it?"

But before anything could be offered in response, Hayes was thumbing through pages again, stopping at still another heavily underlined passage.

"The wise man throws himself on the side of his assailants. It is more his interest than it is theirs to find his weak point. Blame is safer than praise. I hate to be defended in a newspaper. As long as all that is said is said against me I feel a certain assurance of success. But as soon as honeyed words of praise are spoken for me, I feel as one that lies unprotected before his enemies."

34

Hayes closed the book and put it gently back on top of the stack. "Now that pretty well sums up my attitude towards the press," he said.

"Does it?" I said. "It seems to me there's a contradiction between what you just read and the attitude you expressed earlier, that the press, with its essential negativism, was doing irreparable damage to the country."

"*Contradiction?*" Hayes snapped. "I don't see any goddamn contradiction at all."

His mouth clamped shut and his eyes said he did not want to pursue the subject. He sat in silence for a minute, staring at the bookshelves. His voice had become raspy and he coughed hard twice, trying to clear his throat. Then he started up again.

"Now this may sound corny to a fella like yourself," he proceeded. "But all my life I have been and always will be a *hero worshipper.*"

"Which means?"

"Well," he said, "when I get a great athlete—and I've had my share or you wouldn't be here talking to me now—I feel a little tingle inside because I'm a great respecter of the great athlete. I feel it's my duty to them as a coach to get the best out of them, and I get very bitter when they don't want to give us the best, because they *owe* it to us.

"Now," he went on, "you take my quarterback a few years back, a fella by the name of Rex Kern. You never saw anything like him. He was a great leader and he worked at football like a sonofabitch. Rex was also a pretty good student, not great, but good. All A's and B's. I remember one quarter in his junior year he made over fifty speeches for the Fellowship of Christian Athletes. He was truly a helluva great kid, and a coach ends up respecting those kinds of quality kids just all the way. So when somebody starts in with that bullshit about football players being dumb jocks and animals, I have just two words for them: Rex Kern. He's my idea of a football hero.

"Now what really gets me mad is when you fellas from the press and pipsqueaks like that Jack Scott up at Oberlin talk about your *de*-humanization and brutality. They've gotten so goddamned liberal up there at Oberlin they don't even give a shit about sports anymore. I hear they're even letting w-o-m-e-n in their sports program now. That's your Women's Liberation, boy—bunch of goddamn lesbians. . . . You can bet your ass that if you have women around— and I've talked to psychiatrists about this—you aren't gonna be worth a damn. No sir! Man has to dominate. There's just no other way. Now just the other day one of my old players came up to see me and this fella was really down in the dumps. Y' see, he's married to one of these liberated gals. She's real liberated, all right. She'll screw just about anything in pants. And it's a goddamned shame, because this fella is in the category of a genius. His I.Q. is up around one ninety. And I told him there's an old saying about the best way to treat a woman, and that is to knock her up and hide her shoes. Jeezus Christ, I'd like to get that goddamn Oberlin on our schedule! We'd show them what *de*-humanization is all about."

He went on, but the pace tapered and the tone softened.

"Y' see, the football player has got to be a *better* human being than the other students on campus. He's got to have cleaner habits. He's got to work harder. He's got to schedule classes earlier to have time for practice. Now, I've done some research on this, and studies show that on your average

36

campus, about twenty-five percent of the students need psychiatric counseling. But in all my years here I've sent only two of my players to a psychiatrist, and in both cases, the problems had nothing at all to do with football. One kid was an exhibitionist—he used to pull his pants down and masturbate in front of little girls. The other kid got all caught up in religion.

"Now they talk about football players being sadistic. I can only remember one kid here who was *really* sadistic, and I had to get rid of him even though he was a pretty darn good football player. He was a black kid and he used to ride up and down on the elevators of the dorm, turn the lights off, and when a couple of white kids would get in he'd just beat the hell out of 'em."

With a faint smile, Woody Hayes repeated: *"He just beat the goddamn hell out of 'em."* Then he shifted the subject back to safer ground.

"Now by the way, Rex Kern is from a little town called Lancaster, Ohio, and do you know what other great leader came from there? Well, now, it was General William Tecumseh Sherman. He's the man who ran an option play right through the South in the Civil War. If you study your history, you'll find that Billy Sherman's march to the sea used the *alternative objective approach,* striking over a broad front. The defense never had a chance to dig in. Then a hundred years later comes a fella from the same little town, Rex Kern, and the way he ran that option play gave our Buckeye attack all the same offensive versatility Billy Sherman had. Y' see, history is full of such ironies."

The monologue kept going, as if the speaker were unable to stop. What had happened so far was only preamble. For four more hours Woody Hayes kept reaching in and pulling out stories; throwing in opinions and polemics; quoting famous people; bolting out of his chair; declaiming against the press; predicting the fall of America; railing against permissiveness; clearing his throat; apotheosizing football. From time to time there would be a knock on the door and Hayes would go off and confer. Then he would come back and pick up the manic aria where he'd left off: recounting battles and military strategy; reciting his versions of historical events; excoriating progressive ideas; relating football to anything and everything—all in a manner that constantly shuttled back and forth between hushed, fervid undertone and fist-slamming, klaxon-horn rage. Meanwhile there was nothing for me to do but sit and listen, a mute target for Hayes's cerebral panzer divisions.

During one brief stretch Hayes managed to string together quotations from:

—General George Patton ("Wars may be fought with weapons but they are won by men.")

—Abraham Lincoln ("Let us have faith that right makes might and in that faith let us to the end dare do our duty as we understand it.")

—Napoleon ("From the sublime to the ridiculous is but a step.")

—Vince Lombardi ("You can't get along with sportswriters.")

—William Shakespeare ("The evil men do lives after them while the good is oft interred with their bones.")

—George Santayana ("Those who cannot remember the past are condemned to repeat it.")

—John Kennedy ("Victory has a hundred fathers while defeat is always an orphan.")

—Louis Pasteur ("Chance favors the prepared mind.")

38

—Darrell Royal ("Luck is what happens when preparation meets opportunity.")

—Sir Joshua Reynolds ("There is no expedient to which men will not resort to avoid the real labor of thinking.")

—Persian Proverbs ("Luck is infatuated with the efficient.")

—U.S. Marine Corps Training Manual ("Proper preparation prevents poor performance.")

In Hayes's scheme of things, life imitates football. One minute he would be talking about the split-T formation. Another minute he would be talking about Thucydides. Then Nathaniel Hawthorne . . . now homosexuality . . . then goal-line defenses . . . now Pearl Harbor . . . then the breakdown of respect for authority . . . now Metternich . . . then drugs . . . now George Halas . . . then the French Revolution . . . now the double-team block . . .

"Now the double-team block, of course, is the story of your First World War, very simply. Germany was caught in the double-team block between the pressure from the Allies from the West, France and England, and then pressure from the Russians in the East. Now do you know what the Germans did to break the double-team block? They went to Switzerland and got a fella and sealed him up in a box car and sent him to Russia to foment a revolution just so as they could break that double-team block. He got there and he had an innate sense of timing. He realized it was too early to foment that revolution and he jumped into Finland. Do you know who I'm talking about? Goddamnit, of course, I'm talking about Lenin. But then Lenin came in in the October Revolution of 1917 and therein started communism. And who had started it? The German general staff in order to get out of the double-team block."

Hayes was not about to stop there. "All right now, in your Second World War you had another double-team block and Hitler made the horrendous mistake of trying to fight a two-front war. His generals knew it. Just about everybody knew it. Was he a madman? No. He was a totally immoral and vicious and evil man, but he fought a helluva war that killed about fifty million people before it was all over. And in trying to get out of the double-team block what Hitler did was make a mistake we football coaches don't dare make: he underestimated the staying power of his opponent. He thought after he knocked out France that the British would sue for peace. But the British came up with a great leader who pulled them together and they stuck in there. Then Hitler made the mistake of turning against the Russians and believing that he could whip them before winter. He made *exactly* the same mistake Napoleon made a century before. Actually Hitler started out on the twenty-second of June. Napoleon started out on the twenty-first of June. But here again is the story of a man who got caught in the double-team block.

"O.K., now, take your history today. Today there's a great possibility of someone getting caught in the double-team block because there's three great powers in the world—a fourth perhaps emerging, but not ready yet. With three great powers in the world, someone is going to get caught in the double-team block. The trip that Dick Nixon made to China and Russia last year had that in mind exactly. Because I think he studied the situation and he realized there is a great likelihood of war between China and Russia. Why? The Russians can take out that nuclear plant of the Chinese very easily. They can take it, and they're scared of it. Who wouldn't be scared of eight hundred million people—with nuclear power? There's a forty-five-hundred-mile common front between them. A lot of that is relatively flat terrain, in which a good tank division can travel mighty, mighty fast and get the job done, particularly against soldiers who will come up with small rifles and sticks. And so there's a great, great possibility of that thing happening. If you study your history at all, when you get large nations in modern warfare fighting, it's always a question of double-team blocks.

"And I think you could say in a nutshell that Nixon's whole foreign policy is to keep us out of those double-team blocks. That's why I'm so bitter about Nixon not being able to call the signals anymore, because in football you learn when a coach calls a play 'twenty-six' you run play 'twenty-six.' You don't say, 'Aw, maybe he shouldn't have called that.' You're goddamned dead if you do that.

"Now go back to the Battle of Salamis, where the Greeks beat the tail off the Persians. Now doesn't that take in so many of the things you see in a football game? Fear, determination, backs to the wall, home-field advantage—all those things you see in a football game, and that Battle of Salamis wasn't for the national championship; it was for the *world* championship. If you study your history, the Battle of Salamis decided the fate of democracy, because if the Persians had won, the Greeks would have been sucked into the abyss of Oriental despotism.

"All right now, take your Battle of the Midway. It was without a doubt the *greatest* battle we fought in World War Two. It was almost a *total victory.* The Japs lost every carrier they used at Pearl Harbor. We popped 'em all and sank 'em. And the way we did it was simple football strategy. Our

Marines forced the Japs to overcommit their defense. We caught them with their planes down at the line of scrimmage."

Hayes flicked his tongue in and out like a garter snake seeking a grasshopper. Then he was on his feet again, puffing out his massive gut, making sweeping movements with his arms, and suddenly he was reciting Winston Churchill's famous address to the British Parliament after the evacuation of Dunkirk.

"We shall fight on the beaches, we shall fight on the landing grounds, we shall fight in the fields and in the streets; we shall fight in the hills; we shall never surrender, and even if, which I do not for a moment believe, this island or a large part of it were subjugated and starving, then our Empire beyond the seas, armed and guarded by the British fleet, would carry on the struggle, until, in God's good time, the New World, with all its power and might, steps forth to the rescue and liberation of the Old."

When he was finished he slumped back in his chair. He was tired and out of breath but his hazel eyes were shining triumphantly. "Did you ever hear a better locker-room speech?" he crowed.

There was a minute of silence, then another shift. "Here I am, sixty years old," he said, "and I'm not on my way down yet. No sir! I do know that when it starts happening, it happens very fast. And when it does happen, I'm gonna have enough sense to walk out that door. I'll be a sonofabitch if I don't. Y' know, people ask me so many times how I've maintained my drive, my enthusiasm. I think the only way a man can maintain his enthusiasm for his job beyond a certain point is to be able to see his job in the larger context —the *sublime* context.

42

"This to me is an absolute necessity. I see my job as a part of American civilization and as a *damn important part.* I see football as being just *so much above* everything else.

"Now when you think about what's happened in this country in the last few goddamned years you begin to wonder just how much longer we're gonna last. Up until a few years ago we used to take the team out to a good movie on Friday nights before a football game, but this is a real sonofabitch of a problem now. I remember we were up playing Minnesota and we took the boys to see *Easy Rider,* and it really shook 'em up. We played just a *lousy* game the next day. We won it, but it was a squeaker. Now I have my coaches scout the movies we see so these kids don't get hurt.

"Now you take your situation on the college campus today. The dorms are so fucking filthy now, there's so much sex and drugs, we can't even let recruits stay there the way we used to. The permissiveness is total. Y' know I picked up the school newspaper the other day and started reading this doctor's advice column they have and here's the kind of letters they print. One letter is from a girl asking this so-called doctor if she can screw in the *'su-*perior position' and still have an orgasm. Another of these liberated gals writes in wanting to know if it's all right to masturbate while she's menstruating. By God, *this* is what they're printing these days in the goddamn *Lantern!* The student newspaper!!

"Do you know where you can lay the blame for this whole goddamn mess on campus?" he thundered, raising himself up from the chair and whacking his fist against the blackboard. "It's these *goddamned professors* they have nowadays. The kids have *nobody* to look up to. Why, I remember when I was in school some of my *greatest heroes* were my teachers, because they were so dedicated. They really took an

43

interest in you and some of 'em would even invite you into their homes and treat you just as nice as could be. But these fellas they have today leave the student in the classroom. No, sir, they don't give a fuck about their kids. They go home and forget about them until the next class.

"I saw this happen when we had our disturbances on the campus three years ago, and a few of us were running around and trying to cool down the situation, because there was just goddamned *anarchy* all over the place. Most of these jerks who call themselves professors just stayed away because they don't give a shit about the school. I'm still bitter about that.

"Y'see, three years ago we were right on the edge of a *revolution* in this country. Now if you study your history you'll see that every major revolution begins with the *alienation* of your *intellectuals*. It happened in the American and the French and the British and the Russian revolutions. And you almost had this here three years ago with these professors I'm talking about."

The tirade continued. He looked tired but the verbal explosions didn't stop.

"You fellas from the press called Patton 'blood and guts.' But Patton was a great military strategist. He was a genius with a sixth sense for recognizing a defensive weakness in the enemy. If you study your history, now, Patton could have ended the war in September of 1944 by plunging into Germany. But they didn't give him gasoline for his tanks. They gave him *food* instead. Yessir, Patton could've gone right in there because he'd scouted the terrain when he was in Europe before on his honeymoon. But Patton was no good at public relations, and if you're no good at that you can't get along with the press. I've done some research on that and I understand that's pretty much what happened to our generals in

Vietnam, and boy we had some dandy soldiers over there. Patton once said he had only one equal as a tank commander and that was General Creighton Abrams."

Woody Hayes took off his glasses and slipped them into the pocket of his red windbreaker. Then he took off the windbreaker and threw it aside. "It's getting a little stuffy in here," he said. "Why don't we go into the meeting room."

Around a corner he walked, opening a door into a large room with a blackboard, a film projector and about forty small desk-chairs in five neat rows. Hayes dropped himself into a swivel chair in front of the blackboard and rubbed his eyes.

"Y' know, I haven't had a good night's sleep since this whole Watergate mess started. The way I see it, Nixon had to cover it up to win the election. Hell, I'd have done the same damn thing if any of my coaches had done something and I found out about it. *My* first reaction would have been: 'Well, shoot, we've done something wrong but we can't make it right by letting the whole goddamned world know about it.'

"Y' see, you've got to have internal discipline. Two years ago we found out this black player on our team had his grades changed to make him eligible—not by us but by people at his high school. You just can't be too careful about this because with a lot of these black high schools you go in and ask what grades a kid's got and they say, 'What do he need?' Now when we found out about this we just had to let this kid go. But we didn't run to the NCAA or let the story get out to you fellas because that boy would have been made a patsy. Once you confess and let the press in, they make a patsy out of you. You're dead. That's what's happening with Nixon. The press is trying to make a scapegoat out of him. They're *crucifying* him. But he's not about to quit. Aw, he's a real gut fighter. I'll tell you, though, he's really up against it, having to get rid of all his top aides like that. Jeezus H. Ch-rist, I know if in one fell swoop I had to fire all my assistant coaches, I sure as hell would have trouble running my state."

Hayes leaned back in the chair and checked his watch. "Boy, I'm wasting a lot of time with you today," he said. "You're just lucky it's been so slow around here."

It was late in the afternoon and we were still sitting in the meeting room when three of Woody Hayes's football players came in. They were all black. Hayes, making the introductions, pointed to me and said, "This man here and I are getting along pretty good, but I don't think we will be after he goes home and twists around everything I told him."

The three players were Ted Powell, a sleepy-eyed tight end from Hampton, Virginia; Neal Colzie, a tough and wiry defensive back from Coral Gables, Florida; and Lou Mathis, a baby-faced cornerback from Paterson, New Jersey. Coach Hayes was asking the players questions, lots of questions. He asked them about workouts, weights, courses, grades, exams, women, summer plans and dorm life. He asked Powell, who was wearing a heavy cast on his right leg, about the foot he had broken in the spring game. Told that it was improving, Hayes gloated that Powell had been the only player on the team to suffer a serious injury during spring practice. This seemed of little consolation to the grim-faced Powell.

Then Hayes turned to Colzie, the most flamboyant dresser of the group, in a lime body shirt open almost to the navel and crotch-tight bell bottoms.

"Tell me, what courses are you taking this quarter, Neal?"

46

"Mmmmm, let's see," came the slow, barely audible reply. "I got camp counseling."

"Umm-hm, umm-hm," Hayes nodded. "What else?"

"I got pharmacy."

"All right now, hold it right there," Hayes boomed. "Lemme ask you a question now. Do they tell you anything in that pharmacy course about marijuana?"

Colzie nodded vacantly.

"What do they say about it, Neal?"

"They say it bad."

"Umm-hm, umm-hm," said Hayes, his eyes widening. "Now do they talk much about the connection between marijuana and heroin?"

Colzie answered affirmatively again and adjusted a bell bottom. There was a flushed look of exultation on Woody Hayes's face, as if he had just beaten Michigan by four touchdowns.

"Y' see," he cawed, gesturing in my direction, "these fellas from the press say there *isn't* any connection between marijuana and heroin. But I've done some research on it. I *know* there is. Every junkie that has ever been in the history of the world started out by smoking marijuana. And you know something, I can tell in a minute when a kid's been smoking just as soon as he walks out on that field. I don't even have to *ask* him."

Hayes looked at Lou Mathis. "Now you know about marijuana, don't you, Lou?"

"Only from hearsay, Coach," Mathis deadpanned. I smiled at Mathis and he winked.

Woody Hayes kept right on holding court, with no sign of letup. It was getting late, high time to depart, and as I got up to leave, Hayes picked himself up from his chair and bellied up to me. He reached out that enormous hand, grabbed the tip of my tie and flipped it up in the air.

"Now the next time you come to see me," he chortled, quite warmly, "you better not wear that."

I looked down at the tie, puzzled. "What's wrong with it?"

"The colors!" Woody Hayes bellowed, pointing to the blue and yellow stripes. "Those are the goddamned colors of Michigan!"

Like what can you say when you're in Columbus, Ohio, disguised as 1955?

On October 18, 1970, Thomas Harrington, a student at Ohio State University, was driving his 1962 Volkswagen to campus when he was flagged down by a Columbus policeman and arrested for violating Section 2343.02 of the city's municipal code. The charge: public obscenity. Caught up in the spirit of the football season, Harrington had pasted a popular pro-Buckeye bumper sticker to his windshield. The sticker bore the simple imperative: FUCK MICHIGAN.

Judge James A. Pearson, presiding over the case in Franklin County Municipal Court, took note in his ruling of the prosecution's argument that no word in the English language was more obscene than *fuck*. The judge went on to cite the prosecutor's definition of the word as a slang term for sexual intercourse.

But, said Judge Pearson, following the obscenity guidelines of the pre-Nixon U.S. Supreme Court, "we must consider the material as a whole." The judge reasoned that applying the prosecution's own definition, Thomas Harrington's bumper sticker could only be interpreted to mean, "have sexual intercourse with the state of Michigan." This, he said, "is absurd."

Next, the judge examined the question of whether the sticker appealed to a prurient interest in sex, given the standards of the community in question. Quite the opposite, he said, considering "the prevailing mood" of the citizens of central Ohio before an Ohio State–Michigan game.

"Mr. Harrington's bumper sticker," the judge wrote in his opinion, "accurately expressed the derogatory nature of this mood toward the University of Michigan football team and the state of Michigan as a whole.

"Most of the people of Ohio," the judge added, "would say that Mr. Harrington's bumper sticker also had redeeming social value."

Case dismissed.

Had the bumper sticker contained the word *America* instead of *Michigan,* it is likely that Thomas Harrington would still be serving time. That's the way it is in Columbus.

Not long ago, Albert Schwartz, preparing his doctoral dissertation in sociology at Ohio State, made a study of Columbus's connection to football. Schwartz polled about two thousand randomly selected, adult, Columbus area residents—men and women, white and black, white- and blue-collar. Of those questioned, 85 percent said they had seen at least one Ohio State football game in person at Ohio Stadium. Without having researched other communities, Schwartz says he could not imagine so large a proportion anywhere else in the country.

Schwartz also found that football interest in Columbus is so extensive and ingrained that people are "not free" to say they are indifferent to the Ohio State team.

"If a person expresses no interest he is going against huge normative social pressures," says Schwartz. "He is in the category of a freak."

More than 50 percent of the subjects responded that the Ohio State football team was their Number 1 topic of conversation. Businessmen and professionals contended almost unanimously that a lack of familiarity with the Columbus football scene would constitute a serious handicap in their work.

Finally, about 70 percent of the subjects said they viewed disinterest in the football team as "downright unpatriotic." That's the way it is in Columbus.

One spring day in 1970 several dozen Ohio State students staged a sit-in, blocking a gate to campus. It was the era of campus activism and all over the country students were protesting the Vietnam war, too much military research on campus and too little student representation in the university power structure.

For a time, the protest was peaceful. The students expected to be arrested, knowing that what they were doing was unlawful and that OSU officials would probably exercise their rightful option to call in police to reopen the gates. That's how the trouble started.

Several hundred Columbus policemen and Franklin County sheriff's deputies—too many of them poorly selected and ill-trained—arrived on the scene not only to restore order, but also to impose judgment. In addition to the protesters, hundreds of innocent bystanders were tear-gassed, beaten and arrested. Nine students suffered gunshot wounds and scores of others were injured. In their zeal the police took into custody several newsmen and two plainclothes state patrolmen.

That evening, the righteous minions of local law enforcement lobbed tear gas grenades into those well-known hotbeds of radicalism—fraternity and sorority houses. The crying, coughing, fleeing occupants were then arrested for curfew violation.

Predictably, the post-mortems of city officials and the Columbus newspapers were lavish in their praise of the police, while bitterly decrying the "riot of radicals on campus."

Six months later, almost to the day, more than ten thousand Columbus citizens, many of them students, took to the streets in a demonstration that lasted more than nine hours. Traffic was stopped on High Street, the town's major thoroughfare and the main campus drag; motorists watched helplessly as their cars were overturned, defaced and trampled; traffic lights were torn down; store windows were broken and merchandise looted; hundreds of bystanders were assaulted and hit by flying beer bottles and bricks.

It was one of the largest, most riotous mobs in the history of campus demonstrations, resulting in more than one hundred thousand dollars' worth of property damage. Yet this time only a handful of people were arrested by police, some of whom were seen joining the fun. The mayor of Columbus, who customarily answered peaceful protests by deploying club-swinging platoons, was photographed at the scene grinning triumphantly. Ohio Governor James Rhodes, who rarely hesitated to summon the national guard at the slightest provocation—as he did at Kent State University—pronounced it a great day for the state and the university; and the Columbus papers, whose editorials had trembled with outrage six months earlier, casually reported the injury and damage figures under such headlines as VICTORY CELEBRATION BUBBLES OVER.

Unlike the small, peaceful sit-in of the spring, this was a *good* riot—jubilant Buckeye football fans whooping it up after Ohio State had achieved the ultimate, a victory over Michigan.

There are some places where you can do almost anything in the name of football. That's the way it is in Columbus.

Columbus, the nation's thirty-third largest metropolitan area, lies flat and dead center in Ohio, the sixth largest state and the world's biggest producer of hothouse tomatoes, business machines, stoves, nuts, bolts, coffins, Bibles and football players. The predominantly white-collar economy of Columbus revolves around the huge State University, forty-four insurance companies and politics, the city being the state capital.

Columbus is proud of its smaller and sometimes dubious claims to distinction. World War I flying ace Eddie Rickenbacker was a native son. So was former Air Force General Curtis ("Bomb North Vietnam into the Stone Age") LeMay. The late humorist James Thurber, who grew up in Columbus and left, constantly poked fun at his hometown, where today he is remembered by a homely complex of apartments, town houses and shopping center called Thurber Village. The city also produced the first Miss America. But the real boast of Columbus is its powerful college football machine. "The Football Capital of America" and "The All-American City," exclaim irrepressible Columbus boosters—in that order.

"It's the greatest goddamn place on earth," adds Woody Hayes.

It has been said by some that to discover Columbus is to discover America. Others, more cynical, have said that Columbus has yet to discover America.

A couple of years ago, Frank Zappa and his California rock group, the Mothers of Invention, played a concert in town on the eve of a Michigan game—THE GAME, as it's called locally. Taking note of the BEAT MICHIGAN banners, bumper stickers and the rest of the anti-Michigan madness all over town, Zappa remarked: "Like what can you say when you're in Columbus, Ohio, disguised as 1955?"

In certain ways the city has discovered modern America with a vengeance. It overflows with high-rise apartment buildings, split-level suburbs, eye-boggling ribbons of concrete expressways, franchise eateries and massive shopping malls. Yet in other ways Columbus is as small-town as any village in the cornfields. The city is better scrubbed, less polluted and more complacent than most its size. With suburbs, it's inhabited by more than eight hundred thousand people. A handful of old established families—the Wolfes, the Lazaruses and the Galbreaths—still retain a tight grip by controlling the biggest merchandising, real estate, banking and media outlets. While a gourmet will say Columbus has no good French restaurant and a film lover will say it has no decent art-movie theater, an urbanist will point out it has no deep poverty pockets and no seething black ghettos as there are in, say, Cleveland, one hundred forty miles to the north.

Good old-fashioned Babbitry is alive and well in Columbus. It's still standing room only when the Rotarians, Kiwanis and Lions get together under the flag to make business deals and talk about drugs, crime, kids-raising-hell-at-home and the cost of no-good-welfare-roll-cheaters. Recent incursions of Appalachians and blacks notwithstanding, WASP and German remain the dominant genes. "No American city of Columbus' size seems so homogeneous and middle class in every way," political writer Neal Peirce observed in *The Megastates of America.*

Front-page headline in the *Citizen-Journal,* August 17, 1973: OSU GRIDDERS WILL GET MEAT. The article informs us that while the rest of Ohio and many parts of the country struggle manfully with the problem of beef shortages, hungry Buckeye football players will not lack for good red meat during their three-week, pre-season training. Paul Althouse, an OSU assistant professor of animal science, vows that the 115-man squad will get its full complement of meat—3,100 pounds of beef, 1,650 pounds of pork and 400 pounds of sausage, franks and cold cuts. Should the usual wholesale butchers fail to come through, says Althouse, the Buckeyes can feed on the 400 head of special-breed, prize cattle grazing on the school's agricultural pastures. Let the people eat macaroni and cheese. Buckeyes eat meat. That's the way it is in Columbus.

Benson Wolman describes himself as "Columbus's oldest living resident native liberal." Benson Wolman is thirty-six years old.

Since 1969, the boyish-looking, energetic Wolman has been executive director of the Ohio chapter of the American Civil Liberties Union. An outspoken critic of censorship, wiretapping, capital punishment and police abuses, Wolman is more than a political anomaly in ultraconservative Columbus, where even the moribund John Birch Society is said to prosper. Wolman is one of those rare species in town who confesses to being "aggressively indifferent" to the fortunes of the Ohio State football team.

"There is no question that Columbus gains its national identity from football," says Wolman, who himself was raised in a household of avid Buckeye fans. "And Woody is a popular municipal hero because he is the embodiment of that identity and because he expresses community sentiment on a wide variety of issues.

"The football mania has diminished, but not all that much," he continues. "Ten years ago the university used to close all its libraries on football Saturdays. Today they keep them open because of a lot of pressure from some academics. But you still don't see too many students in them during those hours. Football is still the secular religion of Columbus and Woody Hayes is its prophet.

"It's interesting to note that Woody and the citizenry here have always been opposed to all demonstrations by groups seeking change, as evidenced by the way the student protests were handled in 1970. But during a football game, when a referee makes a call that goes against Ohio State and the system provides no redress for the team, Woody is the first one to break the established rules by running out on the field or destroying down markers. That, ironically, is the kind of unlawful protest that is usually not tolerated in this community."

56

In this community only the coach of the football team can engage in acts of civil disobedience. That's the way it is in Columbus.

The last decade has been good to Leslie Wexner, a Columbus businessman in his mid-thirties. Ten years ago Wexner opened a small women's clothing store called The Limited. It was in one of the city's big shopping centers and at first it didn't do much business.

Today Leslie Wexner is a multimillionaire, the president of a forty-store chain empire with outlets in Atlanta, St. Louis, Chicago, Milwaukee and Philadelphia. Some day he expects to see his chain among the Fortune 500. To what does Leslie Wexner attribute his great business conquests? To the football philosophy of a man he has never met personally—Woody Hayes.

"Three yards and a cloud of dust," says Wexner rhapsodically. "That's Woody's brand of football . . . not spectacular or exciting but you practice hard and pay attention to the fundamentals. No razzle-dazzle and if you lose, you lose, but not by much. And look at Woody's overall record—wow!"

No frills. Minimal risks. Grind it out slowly. Nose to the ground. The Hayes formula for success on the gridiron synchronizes perfectly with Columbus's ideology. To be sure, an occasional disclaimer is sounded that the three-yards strategy has all the excitement of a bowl of shredded wheat. But in general its message connects with a community still imbued with belief in the Puritan ethic: that hard work plus deprivation equals success. "If it comes easy it isn't worth a damn." Woody Hayes said that.

The Woody Hayes football code, like the John Calvin spiritual code, rests upon a dim view of the human condition.

Man is weak and error prone. Too much freedom leads to a loss of control and increases the possibility of mistakes. And mistakes lose football games. The forward pass and the multiple offense with great varieties of formations are anathema to Hayes, much as diversion and leisure were to Calvin.

So it is not just that Woody wins—it is *how* he wins. The victories come about by simplicity not complexity; by stolidity not experimentation; by dedication not imagination. This is what stirs the hordes of Ohio State football believers and gives the conquests a messianic aura. The Buckeyes vindicate a way of life, showing the way to get ahead. Just ask Leslie Wexner if that isn't the way it is in Columbus.

The boys around the neighborhood used to follow him around and do exactly what he said. He was the toughest kid on the block.

He was born, of all times, on St. Valentine's Day. The year was 1913 and he was the last of three children, the second son.

He was pure Ohio. His father, Wayne Benton Hayes, was a wiry, intense man, a self-educated educator, whose own father had farmed the rugged hill country of the Allegheny Plateau. The Hayes family had come, six or seven generations back, from County Cork. Woody's mother, Effie Jane Hupp, was also born in Ohio. Her parents were of Dutch ancestry.

Woody Hayes grew up in Newcomerstown, an Allegheny

farming village of 4,500 people, 90 miles east of Ohio Stadium. His father had settled there in 1920 to take the job of school superintendent. The family had lived in several even smaller towns in central Ohio, one being Clifton, Woody's birthplace.

The elder Hayes read voraciously and was fascinated by oratory, forever committing to memory famous speeches and reciting them with grand flourish. Woody has theorized that his father's oratorical interest may have been his way of compensating for his sibilance—a trait he himself inherited. Hayes's mother, a quiet, strong woman, ruddered the family on a steady course. Both parents were adamant that their children get college educations and see the world through small-town Republican eyes.

Hayes's earliest recollection is of being taken to Springfield, Ohio, at the age of five and hoisted upon his father's shoulders to get a glimpse of then former President Theodore Roosevelt, who was speaking on behalf of the World War I Liberty Loan Drive. "There is a great American," Wayne Hayes told his son.

His sports memories begin with his best friend's father taking him to see the Newcomerstown Clows baseball team, managed by the legendary pitcher, Cy Young. Woody earned his first nickel helping Young spread sand around a rain-soaked home plate in between games of a Fourth of July doubleheader. The retired pitcher took a liking to his seven-year-old companion, regaling him hour after hour with tales of the Major League baseball world. It was the Golden Age of sports, peopled by such mythic heroes as Babe Ruth, Bobby Jones, Bill Tilden, John McGraw and Red Grange. There weren't any Alis, Meggyesys, Floods or Boutons running down their sports or their country, at least not in public.

Newcomerstown was the complete small town: main street, butcher shop, drugstore, funeral parlor, bakery, barber shop, pool hall, baseball field, tavern, local drunk, local idiot, local sports star, local war hero and local tough. If anybody filled that last role it was young Woody Hayes.

By all accounts, Woody and his brother Ike, who was older by two years, carried on the traditions handed down from a line of rough, fighting mountaineers. One evening their father went to deliver a speech and found himself talking to empty chairs. When told that a big boxing match was going on, he rushed over, only to discover his two husky sons pummeling each other under assumed names.

"Ike was the toughest sonofabitch you ever met," says Woody, adding quickly, "I could whip him, though."

Throughout boyhood, Ike went about life with the restraint of a Kamikaze pilot. He caught baseballs behind home plate without a mask and frequently came home with black eyes. One time, while clowning, he fell onto concrete from a sixteen-foot diving tower and knocked himself unconscious for thirty-six hours. Though only five feet six inches, six inches shorter than Woody, Ike was the superior football player and became an All-American guard at Iowa State. But his first love was horses. He was a highly regarded veterinarian until his death at 44 from a heart attack shortly after the 1955 Rose Bowl game. "He was the most unique character I have ever met," Woody says.

Hayes's sister, Mary, eight years older, was also rich in talent. She was George Jessel's leading lady on Broadway in *The War Song,* and when the Depression strangled vaudeville, she became the first female radio announcer in New York.

To this day Hayes insists that he was overshadowed as a

youth, last in line behind his brother and sister in intelligence and personality. He believes his obsessive need to work grew out of a feeling that he lacked the brilliance and imagination of his siblings.

"That's just a lot of nonsense," says Mary Hayes North, now retired and living in Boonton, New Jersey. "If anything, Woody showed *more* talent than any of us. He was the best student. He read all the time and he carried around a little pocket dictionary. He was a natural leader, too. The boys around the neighborhood used to follow him around and do exactly what he said. He was the toughest kid on the block."

It was in sixth-grade history class that Hayes got his first coaching lessons. The teacher told the story of Leonidas, the Spartan king badly outnumbered by the Persians at the Battle of Thermopylae. "We shall throw so many spears that we shall shade the sun," an enemy messenger warned Leonidas. "So much the better," came his celebrated reply, "then we shall fight in the shade." The teacher also told the story of William the Conqueror at the Battle of Hastings. When William disembarked from his boat he was so weighted down with armor that he fell headlong to the ground, not a good omen. But he managed to rise to his feet and, grasping two fistfuls of dirt, shouted to his troops: "See, already England is ours." Woody Hayes still thinks of Leonidas and William the Conqueror in those rare moments when the Buckeyes fall behind in a football game.

Newcomerstown had a small black section. After a wave of razor fights and knifings there, superintendent Hayes took it upon himself to show up at some of the teenage dances to help keep order. Accompanying his father, young Woody got his first glimpse of black culture. "I came to appreciate the

62

great physical ability, rhythm and sense of timing that black people have," Hayes recalls.

Appreciate he did and fifty years later still does. Blacks have been among the mainstays of every great Buckeye team and twelve of Hayes's twenty-seven All-American players have been black. The early introduction served him well. Unlike many head coaches, who send black assistants into ghetto neighborhoods to recruit, he is completely at ease in black living rooms and at black dinner tables. Recruiting black prospects has never been a problem for Hayes. Furthermore, the racial divisions that have plagued so many football teams have been kept to a minimum at Ohio State. No one has ever accused Hayes of applying one standard of treatment to blacks and another to whites. He is just as harsh and demanding on the second group as he is on the first. It is a kind of equality.

Hayes's high school class graduated in 1931. One classmate remembers Woody this way: "A tremendously hard worker . . . a good but not great football player . . . the captain of a mediocre team . . . and boy did Woody hate to lose—even then. I saw him lose a game of croquet once and he took all the mallets and broke them in half against the wall. Then he just stood there yelling, 'Fuck. Fuck. Fuck. Fuck.' "

Profanity aside, the prudish attitudes and values common to his generation and background have remained in Hayes to this day. When an Ohio State athlete makes *Playboy* magazine's All-American team, the player can forget about going anywhere inside or near the Hefner empire in Chicago to accept the award. His coach does not approve of mammaries and pubic hair flashed across a published page. Besides, if he let those players go, they might come back to Columbus not ready to hit.

From Newcomerstown Hayes went to Denison College, a small ivy-covered, liberal arts school in Granville. There he majored in English and history—he was a top-grade student —and played football as a tackle, baseball as an outfielder, and basketball as a guard. At Denison he got his first taste of military history in a course that focused on the battles of Epaminondas, Philip of Macedon and Alexander the Great.

After graduation Woody, then twenty-two years old, began to follow his father in a career in education. His first teaching job was at tiny Mingo Junction High School just outside Steubenville, a town known equally for its air-befouling steel mills and brawny Polish linemen. At that time, a young teacher, especially one who had lettered three times in football, was expected to help out with the coaching chores. For his first coaching-teaching job, Hayes was paid $1,260.

In 1937 he left Mingo Junction for a job at the high school in nearby New Philadelphia, where he found a place with veteran head coach John Brickels as his assistant and protégé. At New Philadelphia he began to gravitate toward the football field and away from the classroom. Yet he would always think of himself as an educator first, a coach second. The money wasn't much better than the year before, but that was not important. It was an opportunity to learn.

As Brickels's close associate, he could observe the science of football as applied at the high school level. He learned how to structure a practice, how a ground attack works, and how to bend young players to his will, to motivate through fear.

"A great and wonderful man," Hayes says of Brickels.

"He taught me more about dealing with young men than anyone has, before or since."

Brickels, for his part, did not exactly return the compliment. "Woody was always subject to temperamental outbursts," he told a reporter years later. "Maybe it's because he was smart, quick and a perfectionist. I'd let him know what I wanted done and he'd do it pronto. He lacked patience. I tried to tell him that when he corrected a kid he shouldn't make an enemy of the boy, but Woody had a hard time controlling himself and he drove the kids too hard. He'd swear a lot, and I also told him he was the last guy who should, that it didn't fit his personality, what with that little lisp of his. He kept improving, though, and when I left, I recommended him for the job."

Before departing, Brickels did another big favor for his volcanic apprentice. He introduced him to a young woman. Though extremely handsome as a youth, with broad shoulders, an olive complexion, and thick brown hair, Hayes was far from a ladies' man. Blustery and self-confident in all-male circles, he became shy and reserved when women were near. His notion of a perfect evening was sitting at a desk plotting football strategy or curling up with a good book on the campaigns of Julius Caesar. One Sunday afternoon at the Brickelses' home, Hayes, then twenty-four, was introduced to a family friend, Anne Gross, a pretty, effervescent, twenty-three-year-old millinery saleswoman. Miss Gross had a bachelor's degree in psychology from Ohio Wesleyan University and came from a small German family of rabid sports fans. She enjoyed talking football. The couple began seeing each other in 1937 and five years later they were married. It is doubtful that Hayes could have found another woman so feruciously loyal or so skillful a fighter in his behalf.

"Anne is Woody's most valuable asset," says Hayes's sister. "There is nothing in the world she wouldn't do for him or hasn't done for him. She has always helped with the recruiting and she used to even sit down and tutor some of the boys. Woody's not the easiest man in the world to live with—our whole family had tempers, you know—but Anne has a wonderful disposition. She's the perfect wife for him. She knows how to charm people and keep them off his back when he needs privacy. And she knows her football. She can practically scout a team as well as my brother."

Though he now had the head coaching job at New Philadelphia and had acquired an added incentive, a new lady friend, for making a good showing, Hayes still considered football a temporary vocation. He wanted to practice law. One summer he tried to enroll in law school at Ohio State and was told he would have to wait for fall. But it was still the Depression. Law schools were full of students who couldn't buy a cup of coffee, and Hayes had a regular paycheck. The idea of a law career was put aside.

"Woody would have been one heckuva great lawyer," says his first cousin, Ben Hayes, a veteran columnist for the Columbus *Citizen-Journal.* "I can just see him now inside a courtroom, pleading a case before a jury. He's one of the most persuasive men I've ever known. A *super salesman.* Woody can sell just about anything to anybody and the thing that he sells best is himself. No jury could resist him. Anybody who's ever seen him recruit football players will tell you that."

Through 1938 and 1939, Hayes won eighteen, lost one and tied one at New Philadelphia. In his spare time out of football season, he earned a master's degree at Ohio State in educational administration and qualified to work as a school principal or superintendent. The future held promise. But the next year, with twenty-three seniors gone, the team managed to win only once—the first of four losing seasons in Woody's long and amazing career. After this bad season, he got into trouble with school officials over his harsh methods. Discouraged and uncertain of his life's course, he enlisted in the Navy.

Hayes will say little of his naval career, other than it was a valuable experience. He entered the service five months before Pearl Harbor, convinced of America's imminent entry into the war and of his own patriotic duty to lend a hand. His first jobs involved heading up exercise programs for new recruits at the large naval base at Norfolk, Virginia. It was frustrating. He was like an assistant football coach who helped work out the team during the week but had no role in the game on Saturday. He wanted into the action. In June, 1942—five days after his wedding—he put in for sea duty. By the time he was discharged, he had risen to the rank of lieutenant commander and had presided over a patrol chaser and a destroyer escort in the Pacific. One navy buddy, Rix Yard, who later served under Hayes at Denison as assistant coach and is now athletic director of Tulane University, remembers Lieutenant Commander Hayes as a tough disciplinarian and an uncommonly strait-laced man.

"Woody drove himself and his men aboard ship just as hard as he does his players on the football field," says Yard. "The secret of his success is that he has never been afraid to make tremendous demands on himself and the people under him. He used to beat his brains out trying to learn everything he thought he needed to know to run the ship. He was completely dedicated. In the Navy most of the guys used to try to unwind. You smoked, you drank some beer, you played cards with your paycheck, you fooled around with bar girls when you got into port. But Woody shied away from all the vices. I never once saw him try to unwind."

In the spring of 1946 Hayes left the Navy to take the coaching job at his alma mater, Denison, which had dropped football during the war and hoped to rebuild its program. He would never again be away from either football or Ohio.

The first season was miserable. Hayes was still striding the quarterdeck but his players, many just back from the same war, found it difficult to maintain combat readiness. The team failed to win until its final game of the year. "Woody refused to realize that a lot of these kids had lived with pressure during the war and they couldn't take any more," Yard recalls. "He never stopped thinking football. One afternoon he caught me reading. 'What the hell d' you mean, reading a book during football season!' he shouted."

Hayes himself was attempting to lead by example. "I try to get six or seven hours' sleep a night and I try not to miss any meals," he told the team. "But just about all the time that's left goes to football."

Over the next two years the players learned to live with his compulsions and competitive drive. Denison won nineteen in a row, and Woody discovered one of the natural laws of college football: the direct mathematical relation between victories and alumni donations. For years Denison athletic officials had been trying to raise money for a new field house. Then in 1947 under Hayes, the football team went undefeated for the first time in fifty-eight years. All of a sudden, the tight fists of the alumni began to loosen up. Within a few months one hundred thousand dollars in seed money had been collected. Eventually, an additional nine hundred thousand dollars poured into the school's treasuries and the new field house was completed. As Woody is fond of pointing out, "People always put their money on a winner."

The winning streak opened doors. In 1949 Hayes accepted an offer to coach at Miami University, a larger school in Oxford, thirty-five miles northwest of Cincinnati. Miami had better personnel, a bigger recruiting budget, tougher opponents and a richer alumni organization than Denison. It would one day become known as "the cradle of coaches" because of the well-known names who played or coached there: Paul Brown, Red Blaik, Sid Gillman, Ara Parseghian, Bo Schembechler, Stu Holcomb, John Pont and Paul Dietzel. Brown, in fact, was to put in a good word for Woody with Miami's president in time to help his appointment come through. Later the two men would become prime contenders for the coaching job at Ohio State.

Once again Hayes's first year was less than glittering—the team won five of nine games. "Woody always had trouble the first year wherever he went because it takes time to get to know him and his ways," a former OSU assistant says. The next season seemed to document the point. Miami won eight out of nine and topped off the year with a Salad Bowl victory over Arizona State.

The near-perfect season brought Hayes, for the first time, some press attention and the image, of all things, of an ultra-modern, young coach who liked to *throw* the football. Incredible as it now seems, his 1950 Miami team ranked third in the nation among small colleges in passing. The wild and wooly image was not entirely accurate, because his running game that year was just as productive as the passing, but it makes humorous reading in light of later years when he would treat the forward pass as a leprous relation. Actually, the Miami team was so strong it didn't matter whether they ran or passed. Woody got full credit for the squad's accomplishments.

Because of his orneriness and tightly strung nerves, his decision to go after the job at Ohio State in 1951 surprised some of his acquaintances, who warned him against it. The Ohio State football program was a notorious beehive. The head football coach was supposed to be physical educator, providing young men with lessons for later life in such virtues as sportsmanship, fair play, teamwork and second effort. Instead, he spent almost all his time anguishing over the team's won-and-lost record and delivering full accountings to peevish alumni and booster organizations. They were not the only ones who demanded gridiron perfection. When it came to football, the cab driver, the waitress, the bellhop and just about every other member of Columbus's working class identified with the university they were never able to attend.

To a degree, of course, this was happening all over the country. But in Columbus and most of Ohio, there was little else competing for proprietary feelings or entertainment dollars. Filling the void, football had become at once a vast profit-making cultural enterprise and an outlet for mass hysteria, whose origins could be traced to the construction of Ohio Stadium itself. The first of the country's giant post-War arenas, it had been put up in 1922 by a $1 million fund-raising drive based on many thousands of small donations from alumni and citizens across the state. Thus began, in a sense, what has remained to this day: the vested interest of the people of Ohio in the Ohio State Buckeyes.

The only thing the shareholders asked was a victory every Saturday. In the years preceding Hayes some competent football coaches had fled the job like terrified jack rabbits.

Most of them got in, got hurt, and got out. Few left without being the subject of unremitting abuse.

Typical was the case of Francis Schmidt, a one-time bayonet drill instructor who coached the Buckeyes from 1934 to 1940. Schmidt had the bad judgment to lose three straight to Michigan, so he had to quit before he got fired. His unhappy departure, however, belied his contribution to Ohio State football.

Crude, uneducated but football-wise, Schmidt had in earlier years rolled up victories of such magnitude that he was affectionately nicknamed "Close-the-Gates-of-Mercy." Alumni and other boosters thought he was the greatest thing since Chick Harley, the Buckeye star of 1916–19, and Schmidt had the sense to see his enthusiasts could be put to good use. In a casual way he began lining up supporters to lend a hand with recruiting. Without realizing it, Schmidt was putting together the outlines of a recruiting organization, something new. Ten years later the concept would be formalized in a group called the "Frontliners," part of the machinery Woody Hayes inherited.

But in early 1951 no one could have predicted Hayes would inherit anything. Ohio State was then known as the "graveyard of coaches," and Hayes's friends were wondering why he would want the Buckeye coaching job.

"Some men wrestle alligators for a living," said an article in *Look* magazine. "Others umpire baseball games. Still others munch on razor blades and wash them down with fire. And there are those, the supreme daredevils, who coach football at Ohio State."

Nevertheless, it was a position carrying great prestige and power throughout the state. And Woody Hayes, at thirty-eight, had yet to preside over anything beyond a small-time, small-budget program. Besides the risks and pressures, the office provided vast financial resources to recruit, train, equip, house and tutor players. Hayes would be in charge of a large force of assistant coaches, alumni recruiters, benefactors, doctors, dentists, publicists, tutors, trainers, equipment men, and waterboys—all necessary to a perpetually victorious football machine. For a man who longed to lead his own army like his hero, Patton, it was a dazzling prospect.

Meanwhile, the time had come for OSU coach Wes Fesler to go. The tall, curly-haired, Columbus-born All-American had returned to Ohio State in 1947. He had served the Buckeye Machine reasonably well and it, in return, had given the gentle, easy-going Fesler four nightmare-filled years of obscene, early-morning phone calls, attacks in the press, endless required banquet appearances to defend himself and blinding migraine headaches.

Fesler had lost thirteen games in four years. The big football supporters were complaining, capacity crowds were less frequent, and alumni donations were declining. Worst of all he had committed the gravest of sins in town next to joining the Communist party: four consecutive times he had failed to beat Michigan.

Fesler was definitely not the kind of leader the Buckeye faithful wanted. They had hoped for a tough autocrat who would steamroll every opponent and get a recruiting boom going. But he had become preoccupied with establishing a relaxed, casual atmosphere for his players. "Call me Fes," he told his first Ohio State squad. "I'm one of the boys." This attitude is fatal to a football machine that lives on its victories.

For the third time in seven years, a Buckeye coach was quitting because of, as Fesler himself put it, "Columbus's stress on winning." He left the job despondent and on the edge of a nervous breakdown. "The fans have forgotten that college football is a game for kids, played by kids against kids," a haggard Fesler said after resigning. "Successful seasons seem to be the only thought in mind now, and that means winning nine of nine games or ten of ten."

Within a day or two, the Ohio State athletic board began hearings and the search for a successor was under way. Reading the local newspapers, an outsider might have thought that a Presidential election was in the offing.

The campaign opened with the Ohio High School Football Coaches Association throwing its critical support behind the candidacy of Paul Brown, acknowledged as one of the country's most brilliant football minds. Brown had coached the Buckeyes for three years in the early Forties, compiling a respectable 18–8–1 record before being drafted into the Navy. By 1951 he had surpassed his college success with a string of professional championships as coach of the Cleveland Browns. His friends said he hungered for another chance to prove his genius at the college level.

The Brown bandwagon started rolling. The Columbus *Citizen,* a forerunner of the *Citizen-Journal,* surveyed its readers and found that 82 percent favored the former Buckeye coach. Brown captured another poll of the state's sports editors. Editorials in the Columbus papers were unanimous in endorsing him. Besides the press and the powerful high school coaches group, Brown's heaviest support was emanating from business leaders and several prominent alumni who were said to have raised one hundred thousand dollars to help lure him back.

But there was also strong opposition to Brown, coming principally from faculty members and two key university officials. One of them, Jack Fullen, the executive secretary of the alumni association, was a rebel and an effective in-fighter. It wasn't that he liked any other candidate. He was still angry at Brown for accepting a lucrative deal with Cleveland instead of returning, as expected, to the Buckeye coaching job after the war. Equally important was the hostility of Dick Larkins, the athletic director and a member of the athletic board. For several years Larkins had been nursing a grudge against Brown for signing a number of Ohio State players, including celebrated kicker Lou Groza, before their eligibility had expired.

From the wreckage of the dispute over Brown one man was benefiting. At Miami, he had earned a reputation as an exceptional recruiter, but the Columbus sports pages had not even mentioned his name as a possible candidate. Woody Hayes, however, knew he wanted the job and through contacts he had made at the university while in graduate school, he got an interview with Larkins. After the meeting the athletic director believed he had found the man who could stop Paul Brown's return to Columbus. Larkins began planning ahead to the day the selection would take place. Together with Fullen, he was confident he could push through a fresh face for the top post, despite the expected protests. Fullen was enthusiastic about the idea. Ironically, in later years he was to become a relentless critic of the Buckeye Machine and Woody Hayes's most bitter political enemy. But now he was about to play a key role in making him coach.

On January 27, Paul Brown, who had recommended Hayes for the coaching job at Miami, went into the OSU Faculty Club for an interview with representatives of the athletic board. Outside he was greeted by a large band and hundreds of students and alumni chanting: "We want Brown! We want Brown!" The WELCOME BACK BROWN banners were out in force all over campus. After the four-hour interview Brown went to Florida to take a vacation and wait for the good-news phone call that never came.

A week later Woody Hayes walked into the faculty club for his interview. This time there was no fanfare. In characteristically tough, bumptious tones he told the board members how he would block shifting defenses, how he would deploy linebackers, and how he would change the offensive attack from a single-wing to a T formation. He also promised he would crack down on anyone who broke training, a not infrequent occurrence under the benign Fesler. As always he was the super salesman. "If this guy can coach as well as he can talk," one board member remarked afterward, "we're going to have a hell of a football team."

A few days later the board finished two months of hearings and announced its unanimous decision. Brown was out and Woody, who originally had the support of Larkins, Fullen and few others, was close to being coach but was not quite in yet. His appointment still had to be approved by the Ohio State board of trustees.

The die-hard "Bring Back Brown" forces were enraged. The newspapers clamored for Larkins's ouster. One pro-Brown group met with Governor Frank Lausche and demanded that he exert his influence with the trustees. Some even tried to harass Hayes out of the picture with phone calls and telegrams in the wee hours. What they didn't realize was that Woody Hayes was no Wes Fesler. Nevertheless it looked as though Brown's supporters, through sheer number, were capable of giving Woody a fight he would always remember.

The battle never materialized. Eight days later the trustees met and unanimously endorsed the athletic board's choice. The most prestigious trustee, U.S. Senator John Bricker, arrived late, but in time to throw his indispensable support to Woody. Bricker, the old-line Tory who was Tom Dewey's running mate in 1944, recognized in Hayes, twenty years his junior, a secret sharer: autocratic, disciplined, fanatically hard-working and contemptuous of failure. He told the other six trustees, who listened.

The pro-Brown rebellion was quashed and in February, 1951, Wayne Woodrow Hayes, at the age of thirty-eight, fifteen years after he blew his first whistle as a lowly assistant high school coach, was named full professor of physical education and head coach of the Ohio State University football team.

He was no longer just a coach. Now he was the boss of a formidable football machine.

Paralyze their resistance with your persistence

In the old days they called him "Little Johnny." That was when he was a kid in the tiny Ohio town of Derby, living on a small farm with five brothers and sisters and a dream of becoming a Hall of Fame shortstop like Honus Wagner, his idol. Unfortunately, he was too small, so Little Johnny had to settle for other things in life—like being one of the wealthiest men in America, owner of the Pittsburgh Pirates, breeder of championship horses and chief benefactor of the Ohio State football machine.

He started as a young, hustling realtor, sharing a bathroom with his tenement neighbors. Then the Depression hit.

Not many men made millions during those years. But by persuading some Columbus moneymen that buying foreclosed properties was a sound investment, and by collecting the brokerage fees, he did.

Today almost every Ohioan knows who John Wilmer Galbreath is. They know he changes the face of cities with the stroke of a pen, puts up skyscrapers, factories, warehouses, housing developments and whole towns all over the world, and even now at seventy-six, may visit New York, California and Hong Kong in a single day to check on his holdings. And some are aware that next to concrete and steel, his heart belongs to the Buckeyes. It's been said that nobody, save Coach Hayes himself, has done more over the years for Ohio State football than John Wilmer Galbreath.

Befriending young football players means a great deal to Galbreath. After all, he himself was just a college graduate with a hundred dollars in his pocket when an influential real estate broker in downtown Columbus took a liking to him and gave him a job. He has learned to prize friendship and understands its obligations. John Wilmer Galbreath and Wayne Woodrow Hayes are dear and true friends.

"Woody and I go back to before he became coach at Ohio State," says Galbreath. "He's always been the hardest working man I've ever known. I just don't see how he puts in all those hours, especially now with all the weight he's carrying around. But let me tell you something about Woody—as much as he wants to win, as much time as he puts into it, he's never too busy to help players after their football days are over. If a guy's in trouble and needs some money or a job or a fresh start, Woody'll always try to help him. You can't beat Woody at that.

"You want to know what my attachment is to Ohio State

football? Well, you can't live in Columbus and not be part of it. We don't have a big-league baseball, football, or basketball franchise, so the Buckeyes are *our* team.

"I have all kinds of ties to the university. I, myself, graduated from Ohio University in Athens but my son got a degree from Ohio State in business administration, and my daughter went there and my sister, too. But the main thing is Woody. You just can't turn him down when he calls up to ask for a favor. Especially when you see how dedicated he is to the young people. I'm the same way. I just love talking to the young people and helping out wherever I can."

Galbreath has been helping Buckeye players for years, rewarding their gridiron efforts with jobs that aren't difficult, hours that aren't demanding and salaries that aren't stingy. If a high school football star can just meet Ohio State's academic requirements, he can get a summer job working for Galbreath, in one of his many offices, on one of his many construction projects or at his forty-two-hundred-acre Darby Dan Farm.

He used to be able to do so much more, especially for the poorer families of players. They could count on him to help fill out their tax forms or to find employment for the fathers. He could see to it they didn't get too far behind on their monthly bills. Sometimes a player would benefit more directly. Galbreath admitted giving Vic Janowicz, the 1950 Heisman Trophy winner, money, clothes, a job and a convertible to help him make up his mind to become a Buckeye. Conference crackdowns and rule changes forbidding jobs during the school year ended some of his opportunities to aid the Buckeyes, but today there are still the summer jobs to provide and the blue-chip prospects and their parents to wine and dine at the farm. And the rumors persist that even now, on occasion, he is not averse to throwing his arm around a high school star and promising to do all he can for him.

Galbreath is an essential component of the Machine. He is the best known and one of the most hard-working members of a group called the "Athletic Committee," a predominantly alumni organization whose two hundred and fifty active members in Ohio and fifty more nationwide help recruit high school stars for Ohio State, provide Coach Hayes with strong personal support and contribute money to the football program. The committee, founded in 1946 with one hundred members, used to go by the name "Frontliners" until the Big Ten said it sounded too predatory and requested a name change. But its activities haven't varied much.

Most of the committeemen are wealthy. Some, like Galbreath, are company presidents. Many are contractors, insurance men, doctors, lawyers and judges. Others run government agencies, stores and hotels. For all of them, the recruiting work is a full-time avocation and a labor of love.

Each one keeps his membership in the committee by flushing out and proselytizing the hot football prospects in his assigned area. Most can be relied on to give to the athletic scholarship fund every year and buy tickets to the annual athletic department outings and dinners. And many enjoy doing favors for players—like arranging lucrative summer jobs or giving stereos and clothes at Christmastime or making loans that sometimes don't get repaid. Countless players have been made happy by their committeemen, and they, in turn, with their performances on the field, have made countless committeemen happy.

The committee recruiter's rewards are good seats at all home games, status and identification with a successful football program. As long as he keeps finding and selling the prospects and the Machine keeps winning games, it sure is an awful lot of fun to be a committeeman.

Some committee recruiters have helped land more quality players than they can recall. Such a man is Frank Lafferty, who's in the hotel business in Warren, Ohio. He has been recruiting for Ohio State in and around his hometown since the Hayes era began, and his track record is one of the best.

"We don't lose very many that we really want, and this is a great area for high school football," says Lafferty. "The idea is to keep after them and maybe help them find a summer job if they need it. We have contacts all over the area. Now, Paul Warfield (former Ohio State halfback and All-Pro receiver with the Miami Dolphins)—we got him a job with the state highway department. We got Van DeCree, our starting defensive end this year, a job with Republic Steel. Randy Gradishar, the All-American linebacker . . . visited him about twenty-five times before we got him, but he didn't need a job. His father runs a supermarket. . . . Do we offer any other inducements? Well, we're not supposed to do it . . . uh . . . we don't do it."

Though men of vastly different resources and lifestyles, Galbreath and Lafferty, as Athletic Committee members, perform key functions for the Machine. With every one of the nearly seven hundred fifty high schools in football-happy Ohio covered by a committeeman, it's almost impossible for an athlete with any talent to go unnoticed. Upward of forty thousand kids play varsity football every year in the state and they all have, thanks to the diligence of the committeemen, an opportunity to move on to Ohio State. The better the player, the better the opportunity. But in general fewer than a hundred of them will be considered blue-chippers and thus prizes to pursue.

Texas, Pennsylvania and California might argue the point, but it's been said by experts that Ohio is America's most fertile football recruiting ground. Besides filling two-thirds of Ohio State's roster and nearly one-third of the rosters at the other nine Big Ten schools, Ohio high schools supply dozens of college powerhouses across the country. Ohio boys appear regularly in the starting lineups at Notre Dame, Penn State, Alabama, Tennessee, Arizona State, Tulane, Nebraska, Oklahoma, Iowa State, USC and UCLA.

With at least seventy-five major schools participating in the annual merry chase for Ohio talent and competition getting more carnivorous, it is only natural that some committeemen are not above bending the rules a little. Big Ten regulations prohibit athletes from receiving financial aid beyond what is allocated for tuition, room, board, books and fees. But there is nothing to stop a generous committeeman from lending an athlete a color television set for a couple of years or selling him a car for five dollars. It's not cheating, strictly speaking, just a good business deal for the athlete.

One committeeman, a surprisingly candid wheeler-dealer who has helped lure some of the best players in Buckeye history, is philosophical about the hanky-panky. While acknowledging that it may happen, and saying, "A good committeeman can find a way to help his players," he insists, "We have a much cleaner operation than most places because we don't *have* to cheat to win. Woody has the name and reputation. People know he's a winner and year after year turns out players good enough to go on to the pros and star there. And that's what most of these kids are thinking about, even if it is a little unrealistic—playing pro ball. So we don't have much trouble finding kids who like the idea of playing for Ohio State. It's like recruiting for IBM as opposed to a little 'Ma and Pa' outfit."

Above the committeemen in the Machine hierarchy are the assistant coaches. Each of the nine full-time assistants is assigned an area. Seven cover various sections of Ohio; one is responsible for Pennsylvania and another the East Coast, where recruiting activities have been stepped up in recent years. Each assistant travels through his designated territory whenever he can, gathering tips from trusted high school coaches, and maintains close contact throughout the year with every committeeman in the district.

Since the assistant must know his turf, there's good reason for who covers what. For example, defensive coordinator George Hill, who was born and raised in the Cleveland suburb of Bay Village, covers Cleveland as well as nearby Stark County with its football famous tri-cities—Akron, Canton and Massillon; offensive tackle coach Ralph Staub, a native of Cincinnati who starred at the University of Cincinnati in the early Fifties and later coached there and at Cincinnati high schools, covers Cincinnati; quarterback coach George Chaump, a native of Pennsylvania who coached high school football for more than a decade in Harrisburg, Pennsylvania, covers Pennsylvania; defensive backfield coach Dick Walker, who coached high school football in Cleveland for three years and is a Roman Catholic, covers Cleveland, concentrating on the city's talent-rich parochial schools; defensive line coach Chuck Clausen, who coached at William and Mary in Virginia for three years, covers the East Coast; defensive end coach and chief scout Esco Sarkkinen, a native of Columbus and a member of the OSU coaching staff since 1946, covers Columbus.

The basic recruiting organization was devised a decade ago by Coach Hayes and an assistant coach named Lou McCullough. A short, tough and amiable Irishman from Alabama, McCullough was surpassed only by Hayes himself in ability to sell Ohio State to prospects in their own living rooms. The committeemen appreciated McCullough's work. For years when he arrived at committee gatherings, the lawyers, doctors and company presidents flocked to his side to get a nod, a smile or a handshake. After a decade of recruiting proficiency unparalleled in Buckeye history, McCullough quit in 1971 to become athletic director at Iowa State. But the recruiting army, now headed by assistant coach Staub, remains strong and well disciplined, as McCullough left it.

"There isn't a better organization in the country," McCullough says flatly. "The key really is those committeemen. Their devotion is unbelievable. They go to the high school games, read all the newspapers, talk to the kids, to their parents, to their coaches, to their principals, to their teachers —to anybody who knows the prospect. They're willing to work their tails off, and it doesn't hurt that they're usually very influential people in the community.

"So when the assistant coach comes to a town, the first thing he does is meet with the committeemen in that town to get a thorough rundown on every decent prospect. And I mean it's thorough. Man, you find out everything about a kid right down to the brand of toothpaste he uses. You find out about the parents, too—what their likes and dislikes are. That gives the assistant coach a helluva head start. Recruiting is just like any other selling. You have to know what the customer likes and dislikes, wants and doesn't want."

Finding and selling: the gut work of the assistant coach

and his committee recruiters. It begins in earnest in the spring of the high school prospect's junior year, when the assistants spend four weeks traversing their territories. In their briefcases are reports from committeemen detailing each prospect's attributes: speed, size, moves, arm, statistics, family, leadership, church and handshake. To supplement the data, the assistants send out questionnaires to the prospects, talk to high school coaches, get films of games and confer with principals about classroom ability. The boy's academic work is important. The assistants know that few things make Coach Hayes angrier than losing a player to scholastic ineligibility. By the end of May the inquiries will have yielded a list of preliminary candidates, usually with between six hundred and seven hundred names.

Finding and selling: in the fall of the prospect's senior year the recruiting army swings into high gear. Only then can the direct contacts between coach and player be made. The coaches would like to start sooner—say, in the cradle—but Big Ten rules say no. By early fall the grade reports are in and so are the recommendations from coaches and opposing coaches, from teachers and employers, and, in some cases, from social workers. Meanwhile, graduate student assistants are driving all across the state every Friday night, viewing the candidates in action. Before long the original list is pared to between seventy-five and one hundred top prospects. Then come the months when they will be courted, flattered, wheedled, cajoled and badgered, until they either say no or put their signatures on an Ohio State pre-enrollment agreement. By early April, the end of the recruiting season, about twenty-five will have signed, always fewer than the NCAA maximum of thirty. With such quality, there is no need for quantity.

The Buckeye recruiting army does not wait until the high school season is over to start its assault. Soon after the first game the prospect is bombarded with more questionnaires, personal letters, brochures, then phone calls, house visits from committeemen and assistant coaches. Mail, calls and bodies arrive on a well-ordered timetable.

It is Coach Hayes's firm belief that there is no such thing as overselling. "Ring the doorbells" is his recruiting slogan. By ringing the doorbells, the committeeman or assistant coach gets to know the prospect, every prospect, and is in a position to head off the rise of any potential competition which also might be camping on the front lawn. It's no accident that in Hayes's twenty-three years as head coach, amazingly few top stars have eluded him. Tireless and aggressive recruiting has been the rule. Wes Fesler, Hayes's predecessor as coach, shied away from high-pressure selling because he thought it unfair to the "kids." This hasn't troubled Woody. His adage, on the lips of every committeeman, is: "Paralyze their resistance with your persistence."

There are rules in the Big Ten designed to keep a prospect from stumbling over recruiters during his senior year—and to keep the recruiters from stumbling over each other. In theory, recruiters may make only two visits to a prospect's home. Since the two-visit limit does not apply to people not on the official coaching staff, the rule tends to favor schools with strong alumni recruiting organizations. Buckeye committeemen can and generally do make all the visits the prospect or his family will allow.

Then, of course, there's another way to get around the rules. "Bump-ins," they're called, and they are not infrequent. A bump-in is when the assistant coach or committee-

Wide World

A recent photo of Hayes taken during a pre-season workout.

Woody's father, Wayne Benton Hayes, was the Newcomerstown school superintendent. A self-educated educator, the elder Hayes passed on his love for books to his son.

A young Woody stands on the footbridge in front of the Hayes home in Newcomerstown, Ohio.

Woody as football player, basketball player and, below left, as student at Newcomerstown High School.

Hayes played tackle at Denison College in Granville, Ohio.

Wide World

One of Hayes's first coaching jobs was at the high school in New Philadelphia, Ohio.

Hayes put in for sea duty five days after his wedding in 1942. When discharged he had risen to lieutenant commander and had presided over a patrol chaser and a destroyer escort in the Pacific.

Hayes poses with his wife, Anne, and five-year-old son, Steven, after being appointed head coach at Ohio State in February, 1951.

Denison News Bureau

John Wilmer Galbreath, the real estate magnate from Columbus, changes the face of cities with the stroke of a pen, owns the Pittsburgh Pirates, breeds championship horses and is the chief benefactor of the Ohio State football Machine.

Ohio State athletic director **J. Edward Weaver**, known as "Big Ed," says he doesn't like talking about the football budget "because the figures get used out of context."

Ohio State Lantern

Paul Hornung, sports editor of the Columbus *Dispatch,* goes along with Hayes's edict that local reporters be part of the team—a propaganda arm of the Machine, avoiding stories that could be distracting to Buckeye players or useful to the opposition. Hornung sometimes even wears the school colors, scarlet and gray, in the press box.

All-American tackle John Hicks, now with the New York Giants, is Coach Hayes's idea of what a young man should be. Hayes appointed Hicks co-captain of the team after the players, via the ballot box, had chosen otherwise.

James Jones, who, as head of the tutoring program, is known as "the brain coach." He says only one Buckeye player has been lost because of academic ineligibility in the last eight years.

As defensive coordinator and number one assistant, George Hill is the heir apparent to Woody Hayes's throne. Hill idolizes Hayes and it shows in his speech patterns, which bear a striking resemblance to his boss's, right down to the last "umm-hm."

Ohio State Lantern

UPI

Hayes and President Nixon have been mutual admirers since they met in 1957. The picture was taken in Columbus in October, 1970, when both men were ranked number one.

Hayes with John Galbreath at National Football Foundation dinner. It's been said that nobody, save Coach Hayes himself, has done more over the years for Ohio State football than Galbreath.

Richard E. Garrett

Hayes's office on the second floor of St. John Arena. The walls are crowded with plaques and scrolls and pictures of generals—Westmoreland, Abrams, Walt—friends made on his four trips to Vietnam.

A bookshelf in Hayes's other office in the North Facility. Perhaps the most literate man in coaching, he reads voraciously and applies nearly everything to football.

Richard E. Garrett

Wide World

Hayes at the projector with quarterback Rex Kern and assistant coach George Chaump in 1969. In the course of a year, someone once said, Hayes sees more reels of film than Darryl F. Zanuck.

Minnesota's head coach Cal Stoll had angered Hayes with a series of recruiting triumphs. Stoll's punishment was a 56–7 drubbing in the opening game of the 1973 season at Columbus.

Minneapolis Star

Ohio State fullback Champ Henson, the nation's scoring leader in 1972, suffered a knee injury in the second game of the 1973 season. Even without Henson, the Buckeye Machine didn't slow as it faced the rest of its schedule.

Columbus Dispatch

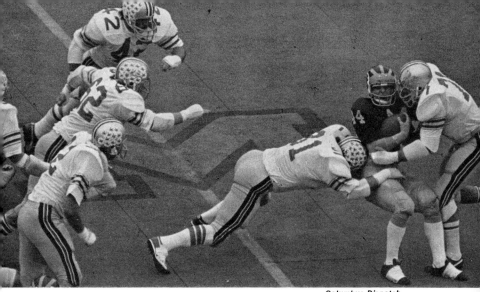

Columbus Dispatch

Buckeye defenders swarm in on a Michigan running back during the 1973 game in Ann Arbor. The game was viewed in person by 105,223 people, the most ever to come to a regular season college football game.

Hayes and Michigan coach Bo Schembechler are equally grim as they leave the field after their teams battled to a 10–10 tie. Schembechler, a former player and assistant coach under Hayes, was more unhappy the next day when Big Ten officials sent Ohio State to the Rose Bowl. He accepted the decision like the disciple of Hayes he was, lashing out at the athletic directors and Big Ten commissioner Wayne Duke.

UPI

UPI

The aftermath of a victory celebration outside Hayes's house at 1711 Cardiff Road. Earlier in the day Big Ten athletic directors had surprised nearly everyone by choosing the Buckeyes instead of Michigan to play in the 1974 Rose Bowl.

Hayes at his North Facility office after hearing news of the athletic directors' decision. The picture was taken less than a day after Hayes, his face drooping and his hand trembling, had said, "We knew we had to win to go and we didn't."

Coach Hayes making certain the Ohio State cheering section is as ready as his team is for the 1974 Rose Bowl game in Pasadena.

UPI

Wide World

Hayes is carried off the field by his players after smashing USC 42–21 in the 1974 Rose Bowl game. The victory was an illustration of what enterprise and long hours can bring about. Not to mention a little overnight mellowing.

This was Hayes's day to celebrate, and throughout it his eyes danced and he laughed exultantly at the lifting of his burdens. Here he accepts congratulations from USC president Dr. John Hubbard, who invited Hayes, a student of military history, to lecture his class on World War II.

Wide World

Wide World

Buckeye history under Hayes is filled with clashes between Woody and opposing coaches, referees, athletic officials and reporters. Flip open any page and Hayes is raising hell with somebody over something. At Iowa in 1956 (above).

At left, he is ordered from the field during a 1958 Big Ten game; center, working off his wrath over a call in 1971; and, right, protesting to a referee in 1962.

Wide World

UPI

Hayes's most famous temper tantrum in 1971 at Ann Arbor. He roared out on the field claiming a Michigan interception should have been ruled interference. After Ohio State was penalized 15 yards for unsportsmanlike conduct, Hayes ripped up a sideline downmarker and squared for a fight with a sideline official (below left). He had to be restrained by assistant coach George Chaump (below right).

UPI

In another renowned explosion, just before the 1973 Rose Bowl game, Hayes shoved a camera into the face of Los Angeles *Times* photographer Art Rogers (right). The photographer, who suffered from double vision and swollen eyes for several weeks thereafter, agreed to drop charges he had filed in exchange for a letter of apology from his attacker.

Wide World

A happy post-game locker-room scene was unusual during Hayes's early years at Ohio State. Woody holds the football after upsetting Wisconsin, and assistant coach Ernie Godfrey plants a kiss. To Hayes's left is Hopalong Cassady (No. 40), who is sometimes credited with saving Woody's job.

Jack Fullen, the executive secretary of the Ohio State alumni association, was originally a big-time football enthusiast and a Hayes supporter. Later he became a relentless critic of the Machine and Woody Hayes's most bitter political enemy.

Hayes's predecessor at Ohio State, Wes Fesler, left the job despondent and on the edge of a nervous breakdown. He had committed the gravest of sins in Columbus next to joining the Communist party: four consecutive times he had failed to beat Michigan.

Ohio State Lantern

Wide World

Hayes stares off into space after receiving telegram from Big Ten Commissioner Tug Wilson placing the Buckeyes on one year's probation in 1956. An investigation turned up irregularities in the football team's job program and Hayes admitted giving money to players in need.

Wide World

Hayes in a solemn moment after losing to USC 42–17 in the 1973 Rose Bowl, the most humiliating defeat in his long and amazing career.

Hayes and his wife, Anne.

Citizen-Journal

Citizen-Journal

Hayes and the late Vince Lombardi hit it off immediately when they first met in the mid-Fifties. Maybe it was because the similarities between them, spiritual as well as physical, were so striking. Though only a football coach, Lombardi grew into a national figure, a man who stirred the extremes of worship and hate. Nobody could deny that Woody Hayes was marching to a similar drummer. In the Watergate era, he is one of the few conservative heroes still winning.

man just happens to show up at the hamburger stand where the prospect hangs out or the bar where his father hangs out.

If all the visits, prearranged and "accidental," accomplish what they're supposed to, the prospect's appetite will be whetted and he will be invited to spend forty-eight hours on the Ohio State campus. For this, the only expense-paid visit allowed, an ordinary blue-chipper and his parents can expect to be entertained lavishly, considering that Columbus is not New York or San Francisco. They can look forward to a guided tour of the campus from the weight room to the library, a conference with a friendly dean or professor, tickets to a hockey or basketball game, cocktails with the coaches and dinner at a downtown rooftop restaurant, usually with Coach Hayes and his wife Anne. Sometime during the visit, the ordinary blue-chipper meets a few members of the varsity, and a player he might have something in common with is provided as an escort to a party where he can meet girls. If the blue-chipper is extraordinary, he can expect something more, namely a visit to John Wilmer Galbreath's Darby Dan Farm.

It's a vast stretch of landscape, ten miles west of Columbus. The walls of the main house are covered with stuffed animals from East African and South American hunting parties. Where the stuffed animals leave off, the real ones begin. Outside in Galbreath's very own game reserve roam zebras, impalas, water bucks, Thomson and Grant gazelles, sitatungas, lechwe and dozens of other exotic beasts. Nearby stands the race track where his Kentucky Derby–bound thoroughbreds sometimes train. You almost forget it's really a farm until you see the 2,000 acres of corn, wheat and soybeans. For coming and going, there's a 6,000-foot airstrip, long enough to accommodate his private jet. Surrounding it all are 35 miles of white plank fences that a lot of Ohio State players have painted for fun and profit. It's the kind of spread that might have dazzled Kubla Khan, not to mention a high school youngster who is just learning to shave.

Some prospects are impressed less by wealth than by sports figures they've been hearing about as long as they can remember. Jack Tatum, John Brockington, Rex Kern, Paul Warfield, Matt Snell, Jim Parker, Hopalong Cassady, John Havlicek, Jerry Lucas, Jack Nicklaus and many other premier, ex-Buckeye athletes have been known to pitch in with phone calls and letters when called on by the Machine. Nicklaus once got on the phone long distance with a prospect forty minutes after winning the Master's Tournament.

When it comes to recruiting, the Machine can sometimes even count on Ohio's politicos. Brian Dowling was watching television one afternoon his senior year in high school when he heard a squadron of motorcycle policemen roar up to his front door. Terrified, Dowling opened the door to find his welcome mat occupied by Ohio Governor James Rhodes, who is best remembered for Kent State and his political rallying cry: "Profit is not a dirty word in Ohio." So impressed was Dowling with Rhodes's salesmanship that he enrolled at Yale. Such failures, however, are the exception.

The average head coach stays close to home during recruiting season. He may range far afield for two or three exceptional prospects, but for the most part he assigns his assistants to do the out-of-state work. As usual Woody Hayes operates apart from the norm. He never seems to stop moving. From December to April he is likely to make eight trips to the New York area, six to Pennsylvania, two to Washington, D.C., three to the South and one to the South-west, to say nothing of repeated forays throughout the Midwest.

The long-distance runner needs a finishing kick, and in the recruiting marathon few men run the gun lap like Woody Hayes. Most coaches will sit on a prospect's living-room couch, rubbing their hands raw, looking nervous and wide eyed, talking nonstop. Their pitch is predictable. They promise a starting spot by the youngster's sophomore year, at the latest, marvel at how he'll fit in so well with their particular offense or defense, emphasize the big money such-and-such ex-player got when he turned pro, go on about why it's better to play on *their* artificial turf and in front of *their* fans and predict nothing but national championships and Heisman trophies in the prospect's future. They harp on technical football, drawing diagrams of their pro-type offense or defense ad nauseam.

The Hayes approach is different. Inside the prospect's living room, with the appropriate committeeman at his side, he is an island of calm and composure. Serious and attentive, he sits up straight, hands folded on his trousers, and speaks sparingly. When he does talk, his voice is soft and low and the corners of his mouth turn up sympathetically.

The low-keyed manner is disarming and it is meant to be. He knows that because of his reputation, most recruits and their parents expect him to be all hot lava and rage. So when he shows up at the door bestowing benign smiles, nodding respectfully, asking light-hearted questions, exuding charm, instead of being pushy and antagonistic or, God help us, breaking up the furniture, the hosts smile back gratefully. They are relieved, if not entranced. And after he leaves, they may ask: "Now how in the world could that wonderful man be the same one we've always heard about?" With that question, ever so common, the hook is in, the sale assured.

Actually, Hayes has two approaches, one for the prospect and another, much stronger, for his parents. With the player himself, he is direct and businesslike, hoisting up a challenge and promising nothing. This tactic is designed to appeal to the athlete's competitive instinct. He is negotiating from strength. Everybody knows Ohio State is a very large school, spends a lot of money for football, plays on television once or twice a season, produces plenty of All-Americans and professionals and has won big for many years.

"Now, son, we think you're a hitter," he will say. "We think you can play a lot for Ohio State."

Then the prospect may nod and timidly offer up the observation that Ohio State might already have enough good football players to keep the seat of his pants in touch with the bench. Hayes's answer never varies.

"Now we think you're a hundred-and-ten percenter, son. You come with us, dig in your heels and prove you're the best. You just have to ask yourself whether you're man enough to be a Buckeye."

This message hits hard. But the real work is done on mom and dad and, with them, there is seldom a mention of football. The talk is all about education, or at least what you can get from one—about how so many of his players graduate, about Ohio State's wonderful faculty, lofty academic ranking, magnificent job placement bureau. *"Ah, so your son wants to be a doctor. Well, we've got the best darned medical school in the country and here's something that will interest you: three years in a row one of our football players was the Number 1 medical student. . . . You say your son wants to go into business. Well, we've got a great business administration program. Oh, it's a dandy program. . . . He wants to be a veterinarian? We've got a fine department there. . . . Law school? None better. And we can help him get in, too. . . . Umm-hm . . . Umm-hm . . . Don't believe what you hear about us being a football factory."*

If the family still isn't convinced that Ohio State is a cross between Harvard and MIT, the educational line of talk will continue, with emphasis on practical advantages and end results. *"Now if your son plans to live in Ohio, it just doesn't make any sense to go anywhere but Ohio State. He can make the contacts he needs and we can help him. And at Ohio State, there's a good chance your boy will get his degree, because eighty-four percent of our ball players do and most graduate in four years."*

The claim is difficult to certify, since the OSU registrar refuses to release the names of football players who graduated with their class, asserting only that "most of them did." And a check of the 1973 Football Register shows that only five of the twenty-four former Buckeyes on pro teams at the start of the season had earned their degree, with nongraduates including such stars as Tatum, Brockington and Warfield.

Hayes will keep going until sunrise if necessary, with the loyal committeeman at his side, to help the boy and his parents make up their minds. Recruiting is the name of the game, and each prospect represents an investment—months of visits, official and unofficial; dozens of letters, postcards and telegrams; and hundreds of phone calls. The payoff comes every Saturday afternoon in the fall when the touchdowns and field goals are totaled. If the committeeman comes through, he will be patted on the back by Coach Hayes and used again next season. If he doesn't, he will be ignored, his name scratched off the active membership roles.

That hurts. "Those committeemen really take pride in their work," says McCullough. "If a company has a man who doesn't produce, who isn't selling enough, they get rid of him for somebody else, don't they?"

Once or twice a year the Buckeye recruiting corps musters in Columbus. These gatherings exude the aura of a high mass with the committeemen resounding their praise of the Hayes regime. The committee's "salesmanship school" every August, with Coach Hayes lecturing on how to recruit and passing out awards, is an exhibition of organizational strength that should freeze the blood of opposing coaches.

"When you've got an organization like Ohio State, you're going to get the top prospects," says Duffy Daugherty, who coached at Michigan State for nineteen seasons. "These sponsors take the boys under their wings and they have the resources to treat them royally. It's become the custom for them to arrange a job that will enable a boy to earn as much as twenty-five hundred dollars in two summer months. The small schools with piddling recruiting organizations don't stand a chance."

Besides the three hundred core committeemen in Ohio, Pennsylvania and points east, the Machine has contacts from Florida to California, from Texas to Canada, and even in Europe, a good place to look for place kickers. Most of the contacts are drawn from the ranks of alumni who have scattered to all parts of the Western world. They don't get to Ohio Stadium much anymore and they aren't official members of the committee. But their memories are long, and it's nice to know they can still contribute to the cause by tipping off the Buckeye coaching staff whenever a "good one" comes up where they live. Then, too, there are the former assistant coaches and players, many of whom have remained loyal to Hayes. They prove it by keeping a sharp eye out for prospects and, when asked, working to get them.

The expanding geography of the recruiting army is reflected by the Ohio State roster. Fifteen years ago, only one of the top forty players came from outside Ohio, and he was from a Kentucky town just across the river from Cincinnati. Today fully one-third of the squad is from out-of-state.

Along with recruiting, another Machine component that has been precision honed is tutoring. It too has contributed much to the extraordinary success of the big-time football operation at Ohio State. The purpose of the tutoring program is simple—to lift the grade-point average of each player to a C, so he'll qualify to keep putting on the pads. And it works. According to assistant athletic director James Jones who, as head of the tutoring program, occupies the exalted position known in football jargon as "the brain coach," only one Buckeye player has been lost to academic ineligibility in the last eight years.

"Sure, we have a commitment to football and winning games," says Jones, who supervises nightly study halls and a team of two dozen tutors, while keeping his speech, hair and handshake in the Marine-drill-sergeant style of the Fifties. "We have an investment in each kid, and if he's a flunk-out, we've lost our money. Okay? But we also have a moral commitment to each kid. Okay? Our revenues from football are just tremendous. Now if these kids don't get an education we've cheated them, because we live off their efforts. And we're proud, mighty proud, of the fact that eventually about eighty-five percent of our players get their degrees. We really feel equally committed to the two goals —the winning and the education. Okay?"

Maybe not okay. A different version is offered by Greg

Thomas, director of Ohio State's black education center and unofficial adviser to a number of black players. "That's so much jive. They hold up these high graduation figures and, dig it, they say, 'See what a fine education our boys get?' Well, shit, when they have to make the choice between eligibility and education, ain't no way they're gonna pick the education. Like some of the black dudes have told me the coaches go through some changes when they ask to take courses that might be a little more demanding academically or ideologically oriented—shit that might mess up their head for football. They want the players taking popcorn stuff like physical education, recreation or business, which are easy and safe and where they know most of the teachers aren't gonna give anybody a hard time, especially football players."

Another major component of the Machine is public relations. Ohio State has three full-time sports information officials and one unpaid publicist, who happens to be the sports editor of the Columbus *Dispatch*. His name is Paul Hornung, and he is not to be confused with the golden-haired playboy running back of Green Bay Packer fame. Small and sad-eyed, the Columbus Paul Hornung is Woody Hayes's idea of what a reporter should be. Hornung is delighted to go along with Hayes's edict that local reporters be part of the team—a kind of propaganda arm of the Machine, parroting the official line, and avoiding stories that could be distracting to Buckeye players or psychologically useful to the opposition.

If Coach Hayes wants to see a certain story in the *Dispatch*, he'll just tell Hornung, "Let's write this one up, Paul," and brief him on needed background. If the story is to be kept out, he will simply say "To hell with it," and go on with other work. Hornung never argues. He's been there since before the Hayes era began, a product of the Ohio State journalism department, sometimes even wearing the school colors, scarlet and gray, in the press box.

When an out-of-town columnist goes on the attack and criticizes Hayes for tactics, temper or politics, Hornung will answer the charges by writing that the detractor is misguided and a fool. Then he will return to the bland player-interviews, official pronouncements, and dreary catalogues of how many Buckeye leaves the coaching staff awarded each player for his work in last Saturday's game. This is news that's fit to print, unlike blowups at practice, weaknesses in the passing game or disciplinary problems on the team.

Hornung is one of the few sportswriters Coach Hayes does not distrust. When a player got busted last year for drug dealing, it was only natural that the coach order the reporter to head off the bad publicity by getting the story killed, just as in a similar instance two years before. What was unusual this time was that Hornung flubbed it, and the city desk ran the item. That brought him a shrill rebuke from Hayes. But in general Hornung's work pleases Woody. As he so often says: "When I want to read about the bad things I look at the front page. When I want to read about the good things, I turn to the sports page and Paul Hornung."

The other Columbus reporters are less friendly, but since they have to live with Coach Hayes, they're rarely hostile. "Nobody ever really challenges Woody," says Kaye Kessler of the *Citizen-Journal,* a talented and affable veteran with a breezy style. Kessler's boss, sports editor Tom Keys, observes sadly: "You go to a practice. You see or hear something and the old man says, 'I don't want to see *this* in the newspaper' or 'I don't want to see *that* in the newspaper.'

95

You make a choice: if you want to cover practice again, you don't put it in the newspaper."

Recruiting, tutoring, propaganda—each a vital component of the Machine. But the most important element of all —the fuel that keeps the parts running perfectly—is money. Since most college football organizations spend more than they care to admit, finances are always a cloudy subject, and Ohio State is no exception. Only Hayes and a few administrators know precisely the amount spent and how it is allocated. As coach he controls the treasury and tells his athletic director what the budget will be, not vice versa as at most schools.

The outlays are enormous. Even in a lean year, when most of the prospects are mediocrities, Hayes may still shell out one hundred thousand dollars for a recruiting campaign. Opponents say Ohio State spends fifty thousand dollars just on its coaches' recruiting travel expenses, which is more than most Big Ten schools' entire recruiting budget. That plus the long-distance-phone-call blitz and visits to the campus—another fifty thousand—means the money going out for recruiting easily surpasses the level at almost every other school in the country.

So does the spending for nearly everything else, as the athletic department's own figures attest. In 1972–73 the payroll for coaches and trainers ran to more than $350,000. Football scholarships cost another $260,000; clothing and equipment, $70,000; films for games and practice sessions, $37,000; meals and lodging for the team, $124,000; and transportation, $37,000. The expenditures are higher than nearly every other school's, and going higher. And sitting on top of what is officially reported to be a $1.6 million football budget, Woody Hayes pronounces it all worthwhile. "Football," he says, "is the most wholesome activity on our campus."

It's also the most profitable. Unlike Texas, Tennessee, Michigan State and other major powers which have recently fallen on hard financial times Ohio State's football program still operates solidly in the black, cranking out a surplus of as much as and sometimes more than $2 million a year.

The money flows in from a number of sources. Gate receipts, or "turnstiles," as Buckeye athletic officials like to call them, are far and away the biggest revenue producers. The Buckeyes grossed $3 million from ticket sales in 1972–73 along with $250,000 in ancillary income from program sales, concessions and parking fees. From television and radio another $250,000 went into athletic department coffers, and alumni gifts earmarked for football scholarships added $100,000.

"I don't like to talk about our budget because the figures get used out of context," says OSU's athletic director, J. Edward "Big Ed" Weaver, a physically imposing man at 6' 4", 230 pounds, who played for the Buckeyes in the Thirties. "I will say this, though. We make a small profit from basketball, but I'd say ninety-eight percent of our income comes from football. We are totally self-sustaining and I'm proud of the fact that we never take a dime from the university, even though costs are rising all the time. We haven't had the apathy that you have at a lot of other schools. I think you'll find football interest here higher than anywhere else in the country—I don't care if you're talking about Lincoln, Nebraska; South Bend, Indiana; or Tuscaloosa, Alabama."

What happens to the football profits? Much of it goes back into the football program to assure its lopsided superiority. Out of what's left the athletic department has enough to finance seventeen other intercollegiate varsity sports, pay the $135,000-a-year debt service on its sports arena and field house and add to its $2 million investment fund. But not a penny goes to the intramural or club sports programs that are available to the vast majority of Ohio State's forty-five thousand students. Some of those students are upset about it.

"It's a rip-off," says David Litt, a journalism graduate who covered sports for a year on the Ohio State *Lantern*. "They always have plenty of money for football. But when it comes to a student participating in athletics, that has to come out of the university's general funds and there's never enough money around. Only this year after a big lobbying campaign did the athletic department break down and finally give some money to women's varsity sports. But they still have to be forced to care about students participating in athletics. Why shouldn't they do something for the student? Business is good."

Business is very good and getting better. It's no accident. The Machine's resources have made it nearly impossible in recent years for Big Ten opponents—except Michigan, also a financially successful football program—to present anything more than quivering resistance on the gridiron. Week after week, Coach Hayes makes his fans happy, keeps his team motivated and shows his muscle for the national rankings by rolling up landslide victories over adversaries who cannot afford to recruit, train or equip the way his Machine can. The undermanned, underfinanced opponents count themselves fortunate to score even one touchdown against him, just as they are lucky, in certain cases, to field a team at all, since they don't fill their stadiums, don't play on TV, and don't get much in the way of donations from grateful alumni. It's a classic rich-getting-richer cycle.

"We smaller schools in the Big Ten just don't have the wherewithal and, as a result, there's no balance any more," says Francis Graham, athletic department business manager at Iowa University. "Ohio State has the highest athletic budget in the country—$4.3 million. Michigan has a $3.6 million budget. Our budget is $1.5 million for all sports and we're just breaking even. We really can't afford to bring kids all the way across the country to visit our campus. Either we drastically cut back on scholarships and de-emphasize winning or all you'll have left is the Ohio States. And I personally don't think college football should boil down to the survival of the fittest."

Graham, like many athletic officials in similar straits, believes the only answer may lie in sweeping NCAA reforms: imposing spending ceilings; limiting or even eliminating recruiting; reducing the size of football squads; returning perhaps to one-platoon football.

With calls for change getting louder, the widely respected Carnegie Foundation for the Advancement of Teaching has decided to undertake a new study of college athletics. The result is expected to be even more scathing than the foundation's first report—the most thorough and scholarly on the subject to date—which found many abuses in collegiate sports, especially football, stemming from what it called "the growth of professionalism" and "excessive organizational discipline." The first Carnegie Report was published in 1929.

Woody Hayes, in countless speeches, lambastes the criticism, any and all, past and present, as "a plot to undermine football" and concedes nothing. "I say again, and I am proud of it, football is the most wholesome activity we have on this campus. . . . the only place a youngster learns teamwork, mental discipline and the value of hard work . . . where the men who teach the youngsters aren't openly encouraging permissiveness and protest . . . And I can't think of an activity that's more valuable. The whole student body benefits from what we do, not just the athletic department. . . . University fund-raisers tell me every time we win and fill the stadium and unify the students and alumni, it makes raising money much easier. . . . We provide wonderful publicity for the university. I don't think anybody will deny that."

Hayes knows that no matter what the Carnegie Report and the critics contend, most people around him say *he* is right. He does not have to excuse himself for any part of the powerful alliance of money, high-pressure recruiting, tutoring and special treatment. The distant rumblings of discontent with big-time, big-business college football are beginning to be felt across the country by students, faculty, administrators, alumni, players and even some coaches. But not by Woody Hayes.

"I don't think many people around here are against a big-time program," he has said. "We have more than eighty-five thousand seats in our stadium and every one of them is filled every game. . . . people from all over the state, no matter what their politics or religion or color . . . they love and rally round the Buckeyes."

It was almost forty-five years after the original Carnegie Report was issued that Hayes got up to speak before a downtown Columbus Rotary Club meeting that began with prayers for Richard Nixon and an undefeated season. Amid loud applause, grim but full of confidence, he said: "Somebody asked me the other day what I thought these so-called critics wanted and I said, 'I know what they want. They want to destroy football.' Well, damnit all, they're *not* going to destroy a very wonderful American institution."

The football tail is wagging the college dog.

Woody Hayes knew he didn't have much time to disprove the critics, to make converts out of the skeptics. It was his first year as coach of the Buckeyes and he wasn't going to waste a minute. He had been given a one-year contract with a gentlemen's agreement for five. But one long losing streak, one bad season, one lopsided loss to Michigan and he'd be looking for employment elsewhere, gentlemen's agreement or no. Only winners get treated like gentlemen. To survive he would have to control the Machine and to control the Machine he would have to win. The logic was as simple as that.

So Hayes shot out of the starting blocks in 1951. Like a good politician, he immediately made promises. "We may not win 'em all but we'll show you the fightingest team you've ever seen," he pledged before one of the downtown quarterback clubs. "We'll never be out-conditioned." Then he talked about a favorite training device known as the "gasser"—topping off each practice with six or more fast-paced laps around the field. Later, in the middle of one gasser, three Buckeyes would collapse from heat exhaustion. And many of his players were heard complaining that his obsession with condition and discipline was ruining his first year's team.

When he wasn't running them ragged he was talking his players deaf. "We set a record for meetings," one tackle recalled. "We had meetings about meetings and when we weren't in a meeting we were out running some more. When we finished running we had a meeting about that too." Doug Goodsell, a starting halfback, told friends: "I'd rather be playing jayvee ball. How would you like it, with eighty-two thousand fans screaming at you while you were on the field and that bull [Hayes] ranting and raving at you when you came off it?"

Woody was trying to get off to a splashy start but the Machine was sputtering. The bitterness between him and his players reached such a pitch that before a game against Illinois they locked him out of the dressing room. Then they went out and fought the Illini to a 0–0 tie—the highlight of a dismal 4–3–2 season that ended with a 7–0 loss to Michigan. En route to the Michigan game in Ann Arbor, a sportswriter noticed that everybody on the team was traveling in one bus while a second bus was following along empty. He

103

asked what was going on. "Didn't you notice?" said a player. "Woody's in the other one."

At the end of the season of dissension, GOOD-BYE WOODY banners were flying over Columbus, and there was talk among certain Cincinnati alumni of raising money to buy up his contract and get him out. Unlike most coaches, Hayes has always had a listed telephone number, and one disgruntled Columbus fan kept calling the house at 1711 Cardiff at four o'clock every morning. Anne Hayes would pick up the phone.

"I just called to say good-bye," he'd say.

"We're not going anywhere," she'd reply sweetly.

"Oh yes you are," the caller would insist.

And Woody might well have gone. But once again, his future *bête noire*, alumni secretary Jack Fullen, stepped in and saved him. Writing in his regular column in the *Ohio State University Monthly*, the alumni magazine, Fullen lauded Hayes for not passing the buck to players, fans or high pressures. "The guy can certainly take it," Fullen wrote. "He remembers Denison where he had two undefeated seasons and Miami where he won a championship and the Salad Bowl. At both universities his first season was rough."

But the next season didn't start off much better. In the dressing room between halves of one game, a halfback reportedly took a sock at Hayes, missed and crashed his fist into a locker. That incident, along with the emergence of a flashy freshman runner from Columbus named Howard "Hopalong" Cassady, seemed to pull the Buckeyes together. They closed the season with a record of 6–3 and their first win over Michigan in eight years. That prevented the axe from falling.

"Why do you think Woody still gets a little tear in his eye

when he talks about Cassady and calls him his greatest player ever?" says Dr. James Pollard, former dean of the Ohio State journalism school and author of a book on Ohio State athletics. "Cassady saved his job. Woody would do just about anything for him."

Indeed, one September morning twenty years later, when Cassady lay in a hospital bed, his face covered with cuts and bruises from a roadside run-in with two Columbus policemen, the first visitor at his side was his old coach. Hayes came in and promptly arranged for a team physician to care for his one-time running star. Then he got on the phone with Dan Connor, a former Buckeye lineman and a top attorney in town. Connor owed a favor, because Woody was helping him get the Republican nomination for a seat on the City Council, just as two years earlier he had helped fulfill the political ambitions of another ex-player, Jim Roseboro. Coach Hayes demands loyalty and gives it in return.

Cassady needed a lawyer at least as much as a doctor. The two plainclothes patrolmen were saying that he had sideswiped their unmarked cruiser, swerved into their path and sped away when they tried to stop him. They also were saying that he was drunk and traveling in the company of a well-known prostitute. According to the police account, when they finally caught up with him, he took a swing at one of them, starting the fight.

At the trial nine months later, Connor reminded the jury that his client's picture as a Buckeye star was hanging two floors beneath them in the City Hall lobby. The jurors may not have been impressed but they found the defendant innocent of three of the four charges against him. Cassady got off with a $100 fine. Later, he sued the city and the two policemen for depriving him of his civil rights and beating him, and won an out-of-court settlement of $10,000. If those cops had only known they were dealing with a Buckeye legend, they might have treated him with more respect.

Even Cassady, though, couldn't help the Buckeye Machine from faltering somewhat in 1953. The team suffered from fumbleitis, an infirmity that still drives Woody Hayes out of his mind. "It's just plain carelessness," he insists. "It's antisocial. No back in the history of football was ever worth two fumbles in a game." One practice episode almost proved disastrous. Freshman fullback Don Visic had been racking up gains through the varsity line. As he ripped off another chunk of yardage, a vicious tackle popped the ball loose. In full view of athletic director Larkins and several businessmen who happened to be watching, Hayes went wild. "Get out of there, Visic," he screamed. "We don't stand for fumbling on our team. Get out and stay out until you learn how to hold the ball." An embarrassed Visic tried to stammer a reply but Hayes raged on. Before things calmed down, the youngster tore off his helmet and hurled it at the coach.

At the end of 1953, Ohio State lost to Michigan, 20–0. The Buckeyes played miserably and it looked at last like Woody Hayes was finished. Again Fullen came to the rescue, taking note in his column of Hayes's monomaniacal dedication: living in the dorm with his team during fall practice; holding seven-day-a-week 7:30 A.M. meetings with his coaches; tutoring and feeding players at his house with his wife's help. "In Woody Hayes we have a coach who commanded his own ship in the Pacific, who knows what it is to be bombed and strafed for keeps," Fullen wrote. Larkins also rallied publicly to Hayes's defense, while privately urging him to curb his temper tantrums and sideline histrionics. The athletic director then decided to ask Lyal Clark, one of the finest defensive coaches in the country, to return to Ohio State where he had served on the staff from 1947 to 1950. This freed Woody to devote himself full time to the offense while delegating authority to defensive experts, which is the way it has worked ever since.

The changes were immediately apparent in 1954. The Machine, behind Cassady and an immensely strong black tackle, Jim Parker, rolled to an undefeated season, capped off by victories over Michigan, then USC at the Rose Bowl. While on the West Coast, Woody proved to be as uncharitable a winner as he had been insufferable a loser, saying that he could name six Big Ten teams better than the one he'd just beaten. Later he explained: "What was I supposed to do—lie to them or tell them what I really believe?"

Such contretemps aside, Woody had a jubilant fourth season. Magazine writers flocked to Columbus, placing him in the national limelight for the first time as coach of a top-ranked football team. The local newspapers, once sharply critical, made one-hundred-eighty-degree turns on what manner of man he was. The year before he had been a foul-tempered tyrant who brutalized his players, lacked imagination and never threw a forward pass. But when he started winning every game, he became an inspiring football coach, a brilliant tactician and a master of fundamentals. The alumni, civic leaders and businessmen who had gone gaga for Paul Brown were now joining in the adulation for Hayes. Brown had never done the things Woody was doing. For the first time in the school's history the home attendance averages exceeded the eighty thousand mark. Downtown hotels and restaurants were delighted at the chance to accommodate the new fans now coming in from all over the state. With alumni contributions pouring in at a record pace, university officials were ecstatic. The exuberant athletic department was busy mapping plans to begin a building program, to buy new training equipment and to increase the football recruiting budget. This would ensure the continuation of Buckeye supremacy. The Ohio State football machine was moving into high gear, and the Hayes era was under way with the chain of pursuits that would always remain the same: spending money, recruiting, drilling, driving, winning, making money.

With everybody acclaiming Woody and the big-time Buckeyes, it was easy to forget that the rest of the university was not so big-time. Then, as now, the state of Ohio was one of the stingiest financers of education in the country. Students were jammed into classrooms because there wasn't enough money to build new ones. The faculty was declining and most academic surveys rated the OSU graduate departments at or near the bottom of the major Midwestern universities. While money was being spent lavishly to recruit football players, there were no funds available to lure top scholars. But the alumni were happy and the state and civic leaders downtown were happy and that was really all that mattered.

After the 1954 season Hayes, too, was elated. He could take it easy, if he knew how, and glow with pride at the miracle he had wrought. The GOOD-BYE WOODY signs had come down and WE LOVE YOU WOODY, banners were up in force. He had silenced his detractors and taken over unchallenged leadership of the Machine. With Cassady and Parker coming back in 1955 it looked like another perfect season in his immediate future. But awaiting him was a land mine that nearly blew the Machine into a thousand little pieces.

The trouble started in the early fall of 1955 when into

Columbus came Robert Shaplen, a writer from *Sports Illustrated*. Shaplen interviewed Hayes, Fullen and Larkins, among others, and printed their surprisingly candid remarks in an article entitled "The Ohio State Story: Win or Else." By the time the *Sports Illustrated* piece hit the newsstands, Woody Hayes wished he had used Shaplen as a tackling dummy.

Hayes had divulged that he was giving extra money to players in need. He said he used the four thousand dollars a year he earned doing a local television show. Shaplen wrote: "Woody insists that he never forks up for a luxury—another narrow line—but it's certainly also true that he makes sure he won't lose any valuable men by financial default."

It was generous of him—the boy who needed a pair of shoes or warm woolen mittens could count on ol' Woody—but it happened to be a violation of a Big Ten rule that strictly prohibited private sources of aid for athletes. The question has been raised: Did Woody know that the gifts were against regulations, and, if he did, then why did he tell Shaplen? Hayes has never answered or even acknowledged the question. His friends say he just wanted to help his players and did not understand the rule. Others say he did understand but was naïve enough to think Shaplen would never print his frank admission.

The disclosures raised some eyebrows in the usually docile Ohio State faculty council, which was nominally in control of the athletic program, and brought Big Ten commissioner Tug Wilson and his aides racing into town to begin an investigation. Woody, like the good soldier who tells his captors nothing but name, rank and serial number, refused to identify the beneficiaries of his largesse.

As often happens, attention to one scandal led to discovery of another. Wilson dug deep into the football team's job program and came to the conclusion that about twenty players were getting a day's pay without giving a day's work.

After a six-month investigation, the commissioner announced that he was placing the Buckeyes on probation for at least a year during which they would be barred from competing in the Rose Bowl. The NCAA followed by banning all Ohio State athletic teams from postseason competition.

After recovering from the initial convulsion, Woody, exasperated and up against it, tried to shift the blame onto the press. When an out-of-town reporter asked him to comment on the punishment imposed by Tug Wilson, Hayes stared at him coldly and snapped, "Tug, Tug, that's all I've heard for the last four months." One morning he began shouting in front of several athletic-department officials that he would never again talk to a reporter from *Sports Illustrated,* or any reporter for that matter, though he never denied the accuracy of the story.

"That story really shaped Woody's attitude towards the press," says Kaye Kessler of the *Citizen-Journal.* "Woody's the type who finds it hard not to be frank. So, from that time on, he just figured, 'Well, fuck it, I'm only gonna get burned so why talk to the sonsofbitches.' He never let his players be interviewed by out-of-town writers after that. And you know, for years he really did close the door on all reporters from *Sports Illustrated.* Now a few of them have come out here who he's liked. But every fall around the anniversary of when Shaplen was here he still says to me, 'This is the day I talked to the sonofabitch.' "

The euphoria of the championship season had died away.

To blunt the scandal's impact, Hayes worked his team at an unusually intense clip and said nothing beyond, "I do not agree with the severity of the penalty nor the manner in which the investigation was made." Meanwhile, he privately cursed Wilson and Shaplen.

He never did or said anything more. No one was asking him to. At another university in another town, a coach might have been raked over the coals. But university administrators were saying nothing about reform. The newspapers, which had criticized him on their editorial pages for not passing enough, were keeping quiet. The alumni were not making any early-morning phone calls demanding that he resign or at least tone down the operation. And the public did not appear to be genuinely shocked. Most people in Columbus considered a little dishonesty in the football program only natural, like rain in October, or sludge in the Olentangy River.

But one man was outraged. It was none other than Jack Fullen, the man who had done so much for Woody Hayes in the past. The alumni leader was undergoing something of a metamorphosis. In the Forties, he had helped found the Frontliners, the group that grew into the present three--hundred-man Athletic Committee, the heart of the Machine. Later he disavowed the increasingly big and efficient group because he didn't like the company he was keeping. As he explained: "I thought we ought to be selling Ohio State to players instead of trying to purchase them."

Fullen was less concerned with the violations that had been uncovered than what had given rise to them. As he wrote in one column: "Woody is a creature of the system. He knows that the stadium must be filled every Saturday to meet the budget of the athletic department. He knows how much he is counted on and little by little his ideals are disintegrating. We'll never be off the hook until we stop worrying about attendance and winning. . . . Take football out of the hands of the sports scribes and the gung-ho devotees of the big time and give it back to the university."

Fullen knew the Machine from top to bottom, having raised funds for it as alumni secretary and having recruited for it as a member of the Frontliners. He had watched the athletic department budget grow to a point where it exceeded 95 percent of those of the academic departments, as it still does. And he had seen the university and the football team become creatures apart. Football players had become members of an elite society, with their special tutors, advisers, medical care, food and jobs. They were no longer one with the university.

Fullen emerged as an outspoken opponent of big-time, big-business football, which made him a lonely figure in Columbus. Month after month in his column he assailed the "distortion of university values"—the preferential treatment that allowed football players to get full scholarships covering tuition, room, board, fees and books, while needy nonfootball-playing students were lucky to get even one-third of their tuition financed. He became famous for his slogan: "The football tail is wagging the college dog." An acerbic writer, a talented speaker, knowledgeable and tireless, Fullen represented a minority of one but a dangerous one. His column was widely read on campus and made its way into tens-of-thousands of alumni homes.

As a counteroffensive, Woody and other athletic officials attempted in their public statements to dismiss Fullen as nothing more than a kook who was antisports. A major flaw in that strategy was that as an OSU student Fullen had won several intercollegiate boxing titles and swimming championships. Furthermore, his devotion to football was such that he had not missed a Buckeye game since 1921.

"All we want is balance," Fullen wrote. "We have small-time support for the true mission of the university and big-time support for football. You aren't going to have a very good house if you put all your money in the game room and ignore the rest."

Another time Fullen sardonically proposed that the school give up all pretense of amateurism, hire a professional team and control it under a bureau of football. In a column entitled "Summa cum Shame" he suggested that band members and cheerleaders be given financial assistance because they helped fill the stadium too. Woody's answer was: "It's a shame for a man on our campus to say we have a bunch of pros. It's a damn lie. He is the greatest exponent of the half-truth I have ever seen in my life."

While Hayes was on the defensive, Fullen stayed on the attack, hammering at abuses in the Machine and criticizing Woody for altercations with opposing coaches, referees, athletic officials and reporters. Fullen was kept busy. Hardly a Saturday passed when there wasn't something to write about.

One week, against Indiana, Woody rumbled out to the middle of the field—a violation—to argue an interference call with a referee. The alumni magazine reported the episode with a photographic essay of Hayes, kicking, flailing his arms and screaming. The caption: "The Gentle Art of Teaching."

Another week, after losing to USC in a regular season game, Hayes had a run-in with a West Coast writer who had somehow gained entry to the Buckeye locker room. He shoved the reporter against a wall, then flattened him with a left hook. When the dazed newspaperman regained his feet, Woody pushed him out the door.

Yet another week, Hayes collided with Iowa coach Forest Evashevski. Before a game in Iowa City, Woody charged that Evashevski had allowed the stadium grass to grow too long, in order to foul up the Buckeye running attack. When he threatened to get a lawnmower and cut it himself, Evashevski called him "a disgrace to football," and Woody challenged him to fight. The two brawny men shouted at each other and until Evashevski stomped away, their aides feared they would come to blows.

Buckeye history under Hayes is filled with such clashes. Flip open any page and Woody is raising hell with somebody over something.

In addition to Hayes's conduct, Fullen had grown disenchanted with the traditional postseason extravaganza known as the Rose Bowl. In 1958 the Buckeyes had gone to Pasadena and beaten a team from Oregon, 10–7. As usual, the game was a huge financial success, but not for the two schools involved. Gate receipts amounted to nearly a half-million dollars, radio and television rights brought in another half-million, so the total take should have been close to a million dollars. But after all deductions—including the rental of the Rose Bowl, the shares of the two conferences and the expenses of Ohio State's official representatives—OSU's net profit amounted to only a little more than fifteen thousand dollars. That's the kind of money the school made selling peanuts on an ordinary Saturday at Ohio Stadium.

When the figures came out, Fullen had a bread-and-butter issue. Why should Ohio State help fill the pockets of West Coast businessmen and promoters? Where were the large revenues the athletic department was always talking about when called on to justify the size of the football program?

The arguments won little sympathy among supporters of the Machine, but in the Ohio State faculty council—composed of administration officials and elected representatives from every undergraduate branch of the university—anti–Rose Bowl sentiment was slowly building. The Buckeyes had finished the 1961 season with an 8–0–1 record. They had won the Big Ten championship and the Number 1 ranking in the UPI poll. All over Ohio delirious boosters were making plane and hotel reservations for Pasadena. But the team and its fans were in for a rude awakening. In a tense ninety-minute session, the faculty council voted by a slim 28–25 margin against the school's participation in the New Year's Day gala.

"There were two levels of opposition," recalls Marvin Fox, the professor of philosophy who led the anti–Rose Bowl forces. "Most were against the Rose Bowl in particular. And certainly the main objection was the adverse economics. But there was another objection that the Rose Bowl seriously interfered with the academic work of the university. The opening of winter quarter would have to be delayed because half the students wouldn't be here. The end of fall quarter would also be messed up with people making plans to go. The administrative offices were always disrupted by the Rose Bowl.

"Then there was a smaller group like myself who felt a big football program had nothing to do with the university. We were not *against* football. We just thought it was wrong to spend the amount of time, resources, energy and personnel that were being spent. We were also concerned about our image. Here we were a large and important university presenting ourselves to the state of Ohio, the academic world and the public not as a center of learning but as a great football team."

The pro–Rose Bowl members of the council argued that there was nothing wrong with having a winning team, that participation in the game would enhance the school's reputation and that the council should not deny the football team the honor it so richly deserved. When the debate got bitter, they said that the teachers against the trip were just envious because the football team was getting all the headlines and recognition. To which Richard Armitage, a graduate school dean and specialist in Romance languages, replied: "Give me eighty full scholarships and I'll recruit the best Spanish students from Ohio high schools. Provide me with unlimited facilities and I'll deliver a Spanish team that will beat the University of Buenos Aires, the University of Mexico and the University of Madrid in four years."

The night after the vote, rioting broke out, Columbus's first major outburst of civic unrest and until that time probably one of the biggest mass demonstrations to take place anywhere in the country. In the cause of football, ten thousand irate protesters, many of them students, marched on the faculty club at the center of campus, lofting bricks and bottles through windows and overturning cars.

It was nasty. Those who weren't indulging in property damage were waving signs that conveyed the depth of their passion: ROSES FOR THE BUCKS; POISON FOR THE FACULTY and OHIO STATE TO THE ROSE BOWL; FACULTY COUNCIL TO THE TOILET BOWL. Fullen, Fox and other well-known anti–Rose Bowl figures were hanged in effigy at the school gates and could count themselves lucky to get off so lightly. Then the mob surged down High Street more than two miles to the state capitol downtown, wreaking more havoc and tying up traffic through the night. Miraculously, nobody was hurt. The riot came only a few days after athletic director Larkins had told the council that football was "nothing more than a popular extracurricular activity at Ohio State."

Woody Hayes was driving to Cleveland to speak at an alumni dinner when he heard the news of the faculty decision on his car radio. By the time he arrived he was in a full-blown rage. "For eleven years we have been the victim of a poison pen on the campus," he told the alumni, forgetting for the moment the early endorsements he had received from Fullen. "No team has ever been the subject of such abuse on its own campus as we have during that period. That's why our teams are great."

Then he added: "I understand there are some demonstrations going on in Columbus this evening and I guarantee you there will be no football players involved." Woody went even further than that, ordering some of his players out on campus to help quell disturbances. His sense of public relations never stopped working.

On the second night the faculty club was hit again, this time by a smaller crowd. Protesters started a bonfire on High Street in front of the student union, chanting, "No Rose Bowl; no classes." Several policemen were hurt and state highway patrolmen were called in. On the third night, university officials closed the campus and threatened suspensions and expulsions for students taking part in the demonstrations.

With characteristic objectivity and good taste, the Columbus *Dispatch* published on its front page the names, addresses, rank and salaries of the faculty members who supposedly had voted against the Rose Bowl. Since the council vote had been conducted by secret ballot, the newspaper had to guess about the positions of some of the more quiet members and there were inaccuracies. The identified professors, some of whom had actually voted in favor of the trip, spent weeks afterward answering threatening and obscene phone calls that came at every hour of the night. They also got a lot of letters. Fullen, of course, though not a council member, was the principal target of the slings and arrows. One letter, addressed to Mrs. Fullen, said, "Why don't you have that jackeroffer wipe off his drawers?" Another envelope that arrived at the Fullen home contained a feces-stained piece of toilet paper.

"The disappointment," complained the *Dispatch* in a full-page editorial, "comes as the finale of one of the finest football seasons here in the Columbus community which has fostered college football as one of the finest traditions of academic life and nurtured the facilities which make it possible. Really what did the denial accomplish? Will Ohio State be better off as a result? Only in over-sensitive minds."

Replied Fullen: "More scholarships for journalism students would produce editorial writers who were less gullible."

But the Machine was fighting back. Hayes appeared on his weekly television show, which runs throughout the football season, and launched into a diatribe calling for Fullen's removal. "The only thing that worries me above all else here is that there is only one man in this whole affair . . . one man only who resorted this fall to personal resentment and personal attacks and calling football players professionals . . . when anyone knows they're not . . . and resorting to personal attacks and using the magazine of which he is editor to attack unduly . . ."

Fullen, he seemed to be saying, was responsible for the people who had smashed in the windows of the faculty club, who had overturned cars, who had made harassing phone calls.

"I do want to ask a couple of questions about the man who has brought so much trouble to the university," Hayes went on. "Now if this man is not popular—so many times the question is asked—well, how does he stay in office? . . ."

A week later Fullen was given a chance by the TV station to air his side of the story. "Now hear this," he said. "I am proud to have been pilloried for standing up for the highest in standards and ideals of my beloved university. Mrs. Fullen and I still think it is worth all the filthy letters we've received at our home and unspeakable profane phone calls far into the night. Frankly, although I may be a handy whipping boy for a viciously inspired campaign, I am not important. I'll tell you what is important—and the only thing that is or has ever been important—the Ohio State University. Which is being dragged through the mire. And only because its faculty made what they regarded as a responsible educational decision."

The battle was now out in the open, splitting the university into Hayes and Fullen camps. With his usual heavy schedule of speaking engagements around the state, Woody pressed the attack. "I'm going to learn why that man representing the university has so much power," he told an alumni gathering in Toledo. "I also want to know why this man has a lifetime lease on his job."

In January, 1962, the eleven directors of the board of the alumni association, who had the power to fire Fullen, met

119

and gave him a unanimous vote of confidence. Furious, a group of alumni headed by John Cole, a wealthy Dayton businessman, formed the Committee for the Advancement of Ohio State University. Their definition of advancement was getting rid of Fullen.

In May, with four of the eleven board directors' seats up for grabs in the annual elections, the alumni rank-and-file showed just where their sentiments lay. The Cole committee's candidates won a clean sweep, crushing the pro-Fullen slate. Now, the question was—would the faculty council, in view of popular opinion, lift its ban on the Bowl game?

The answer came a couple of months later. Again the council members from the liberal arts departments strongly opposed the postseason trip. But they weren't enough. As expected, the pro–Rose Bowl forces made a powerful showing among representatives of the so-called land-grant areas of the university—agriculture, home economics, veterinary medicine and, of course, physical education. This time there was much more Rose Bowl support from representatives of the administration. The absence of the traditional all-expense-paid California trip for administrators and their wives had clearly made their hearts grow fonder. Most decisive in the turnabout were the fifteen newly elected council members, all of whom voted to reverse the previous decision. During the year-long interim, the Machine had worked effectively to make sure only supporters got onto the council. The vote was 36–20 and once again Woody Hayes and his Buckeyes would be able to go west whenever they were worthy.

The next day the *Dispatch* reflected on the council's new-found wisdom. "Despite the charges of some last-ditch opponents of Rose Bowl participation that the faculty council would be yielding under pressure, we doubt that this was the

120

deciding factor," the newspaper said in an editorial. "We have the feeling also that this was a much more reasoned decision than the one last year which was reached at a figurative eleventh-hour session in a somewhat emotionally charged atmosphere. Faculty council members have had the advantage of nearly a year's time to reconsider the issue in their own minds, to hear animated discussions of the subject on campus and in the press and to come to a considered conclusion."

Meanwhile, Fullen reminded his readers that the faculty members also had a year to remember what the *Dispatch* had done to those who were supposed to have voted no.

But the revolt against the Machine was petering out. Blocking the Rose Bowl trip had been an attempt to reassert the academic priorities of Ohio State. That it succeeded for so brief a time dramatically pointed up where the real power of the university resided.

The antifootball faction of the faculty was again entombed, its partisans silenced. For a year Woody had suffered. Blue-chip recruiting prospects were hesitant to enroll in a school where they might be denied the headlines and glamor of postseason competition. But he had shelved the detractors, purged the critics and whipped the Machine into line. The high school stars were coming once again to Ohio State.

Fullen was still shouting, but few people were listening. Somehow the alumni secretary managed to hold on to his position until his retirement in 1967. Each year he would scrape together the alumni board support he needed to keep going. He insisted he was retiring on his own terms and in his own time. He was sixty-five and wanted to ease up, he said. But for a long time rumors persisted that his wings had

121

finally been clipped by Woody, who had deftly swung the balance of the board in his favor. Fullen might have collapsed anyway under the weight of the threats and frustration of seeing his faculty support sag and the Machine grow bigger year by year.

Now living in Florida, Fullen looks back and grimly concedes that the years of stabbing at the Machine appear to have been wasted motion. "We lost the Rose Bowl battle and we lost the war to scale down the program, so how can I tell you we won anything?" he says. "But the big loser is Ohio State University. Sure there've been some gains academically. But the sideshow is still the main attraction and the stuff under the tent is of secondary importance. All we wanted to do was reduce the pressure and make it an integral part of the university instead of what it is: a professional athletic empire with a different set of values from the rest of the school. And it's getting worse. For years the NCAA wouldn't allow freshmen to play varsity football. Now the freshmen are playing. For years the Big Ten prohibited red-shirting (letting a man play his fifth year of college, if he has not used up his eligibility). Now red-shirting is permitted in the conference. Scholastic requirements have been relaxed too. The sideshow is bigger than ever and there's no stopping it, because, brother, we like to win. I read recently a speech by our new university president, Harold Enarson, in which he said that one of his major responsibilities was to defend winning football coaches. Now would you please tell me what the hell kind of responsibility is that for a university president?"

Does Fullen see any way in which the university is benefiting from its football program?

"Oh, no doubt about it. Some positive goods do come out

of football. It's a common denominator around which a lot of people can rally and it's a great catalyzer of alumni enthusiasm. And it may well be, as the athletic department is always saying, that if we didn't have it in such a big way, a lot less money would be coming in. It's debatable but let's concede the point. My question is—is it worth the price? Is it worth it to have the distortion of values? I used to sit on the scholarship committee and time and again we'd scrape around to try and get some money for a bright, young law prospect or a physicist. But there was never any trouble getting money for an athlete. We have unlimited funds for recruiting top football players. Wouldn't we be better off recruiting top professors and students? Who knows how many scholars have stayed away from Ohio State because of our image as a full-blown football machine? I think we've been hurt by that image. I know we have."

As for the man who sits alone atop the Machine, his old enemy, Fullen's retrospective appraisal is surprisingly free of bile.

"My quarrel was never really with Woody Hayes the man, though you'd never get him to believe that. Woody himself is one of the world's most honest men. I'm convinced that after he got into trouble that one time, he ran as clean an operation as you can under the circumstances. Woody takes a sincere interest in his kids. I don't think you can question that he wants his players to graduate and get an education. But he's also not without guile. As the job evolved, he realized that there was more to it than coaching: that it was public relations and imagery too. So he started talking up his 'quality boys' and 'building character.' I'm sure he believed it but it was also good P.R.—something to offset the temper tantrums that got him in trouble.

"I wasn't going after Woody so much as the status of the football team as most favored nation. If you're going to give a scholarship to a football player, you've got to give it to everybody. If you're giving summer jobs to players, give them to everybody. If you're running a tutorial program where the athlete is watched, cuddled, indulged and advised, do it for everybody.

"But Woody sees the football player as something above the rest of the university. He brags about how few of them drop out compared with other students. Well, that isn't fair because most kids who drop out do it for financial reasons. The football player doesn't have that problem. And he has a hell of a motivation to stay in school that the ordinary student doesn't have.

Woody Hayes the man is such a strange contradiction of qualities, you can't really catalogue him. He does take a sincere interest in the welfare of his kids but he'll also bully them and smack them around if they don't produce on the field. Next to losing, the thing he hates most is being crossed. He can be really vindictive and violent. But he is also one of the most literate and articulate men in coaching. When he wants to he could charm a bird off a tree. He's a complex institution, all right—a real Jekyll and Hyde. I'll tell you one thing though. If I wanted to win football games, I'd go out and hire Woody Hayes as coach. I don't think there's ever been a better one."

And what does Woody Hayes think, in retrospect, of Jack Fullen? Publicly, he has not in recent years addressed himself to the subject and has not allowed it to be brought up. But in private the mere mention of the name triggers, even now, a wild rage. "That dirty sonofabitch . . . that bastard . . . that old prick . . ." he will shout. "He was just using the football issue to campaign for university president. I made goddamn sure he didn't get near it."

In Fullen's replacement, Richard Mall, Hayes had someone more to his liking, someone he could call on the phone. Under Mall's editorship, Woody could now pick up the alumni magazine and find the kind of articles he wanted to read—flowery tributes to his team and recitations of his accomplishments: the national championships; the record-winning streaks in the Big Ten; the Rose Bowl victories; the new attendance records. Mall would go along whenever Woody asked him to do something and, after Mall died, his successor would do the same.

With the dissidents out of the way, the Machine was running smoothly again and growing faster than ever. Since Fullen's retirement in 1967, the recruiting budget had tripled, but who could complain? The dividends were posted right up there on the scoreboard every Saturday afternoon for all to see. It took a dynamic machine to bring in, year after year, the likes of Warfield, Snell, Tatum, Brockington, Kern, Griffin, Hicks and Gradishar. And everybody knew it was *his* Machine.

Wherever Woody Hayes turned in the Ohio State community, he was being lauded as a coaching genius, one of the few men who could keep his football team victorious and profitable while most other college football officials were losing the moral and economic battle for survival. When he wasn't being commended for his recruiting, he was being saluted for his fund-raising and his ability to motivate. This was the man, university officials and prominent alumni agreed, who had the right solutions, who understood how to get what he wanted, who, almost uniquely among college coaches, was consistently delivering, who, year after year, was *winning*.

As Woody himself so often says: "We make no apologies for winning or for aiming our entire program towards that goal." And, as the 1973 season began, with Jack Fullen long gone and no audible opposition around, no one was asking him to apologize.

7

So we think we'll have a pretty good football team.

A grainy film clip appears on the television screen. It shows Wayne Woodrow Hayes and his Ohio State Buckeyes storming out of their locker room and across the football field just before kickoff. Coach Hayes is at the head of the pack. In the background the Ohio State marching band booms out the school fight song, "The Buckeye Battle Cry." Moments later, an announcer's voice breaks in.

ANNOUNCER: *Good evening, ladies and gentlemen, and welcome to* The Woody Hayes Show *starring the coach of the Buckeyes, Woody Hayes.* The Woody Hayes Show *is brought to you by the Grange Mutual Company and the Grange Life*

127

Insurance Company—your partners in protection. Now, here's Channel Ten's sports director, Ted Mullins.

MULLINS: *Good evening. It hardly seems possible that the college football season opened today, but it did. And next Saturday the Buckeyes of Ohio State will be hosting the Golden Gophers of Minnesota in their opener. Through the heat of the past few days, the Buckeyes have been hard at work in preparation for the new season. We'll be talking to Coach Woody Hayes and some of the players about this coming season in just a moment, after this time out for the Grange Mutual Company.* (Commercial)

It's a Columbus institution. For twenty-three years it's been a staple of the Saturday night social scene in the fall, the most popular late-hour television show in central Ohio, with double the audience of Johnny Carson. At this moment, about one hundred twenty-five thousand viewers are tuned in, as they will be every Saturday night at 11:30 all season long.

The format, like the central figure, hasn't changed much in those twenty-three years. Just as at the beginning, *The Woody Hayes Show* is still thirty minutes long, live, unrehearsed and conducted like a kindergarten class, especially when Coach Hayes interviews his players. The show is less predictable after a loss. That's when the performance of a referee may get more attention than either team.

Tonight, September 8, is the first show of the 1973 season. The opening game at home against Minnesota is a week away.

MULLINS: *You'll be talking about the game against Minnesota, the first opponent, Coach. It hardly seems possible it's time to go already. Have you had a good practice so far this fall?*

128

HAYES: *Yes, I think so. We came back in better shape than we've been any year yet. I think right now we're tired and we were a little bit dull today in our scrimmage. But our hard practice is behind us now and we'll get sharp for the ball game.*

MULLINS: *What kind of ideas about what you had to accomplish did you take into this fall practice this year?*

HAYES: *Well, we looked at it a little differently this year, inasmuch as our boys had played so much last year, had a good spring practice, and had played in a game after the season in the Rose Bowl which afforded us some sixteen additional practices. And it looks now as though there will not be a single freshman in the starting lineup. So these men have all had a lot of experience. We're trying to move faster and put in more offense and cover more ground because we felt they could do it faster.*

MULLINS: *What kind of an effect then does spring practice have in going into the fall?*

HAYES: *Well, we think spring practice is very important. Those twenty days you can get yourself up and we did a lot of hitting and scrimmaging this spring—about seven scrimmages in all. So far this fall we've had only two and today fortunately we had no injuries of consequence at all. And because of that, we're sure not going to take any more chances.*

Columbus and Ohio State—in the college football business together since 1890—have grown accustomed to powerful teams. And during his remarkable career as coach, Woody Hayes has offered up four of the best in college football history: the Hopalong Cassady–Jim Parker team of 1954, which was 10–0; the Bob White team of 1957, which was 9–1; the Bob Ferguson team of 1961, which was 8–0–1; and the Rex Kern–Jack Tatum team of 1968, which was 10–0. Each was rewarded with a national championship of one kind or another. Now as the 1973 season approached, the word was out around town and campus that this squad would be another one of those legendary teams, perhaps the most perfect product the Machine had ever turned out.

There were several reasons for confidence. The Buckeyes had 19 of 22 starters and 45 lettermen back from the previous year's twice-beaten, Big Ten cochampions. Statistically, they were returning 262 of their 280 points, 2,756 of their 2,993 rushing yards and 741 of their 966 tackles—numbers which added up not only to experience and depth, but also to a distinguished past. Besides those attributes, there was an exceptional linebacking corps that had pro scouts enthralled, a young and impressive collection of running backs, and a big and durable offensive line stamped in the Hayes mold. Above all, the team was what football coaches call "motivated": hungry for retribution after closing the year with a 42–17 Rose Bowl loss to USC, the most humiliating defeat on Woody Hayes's 149–49–7 Ohio State record. It was no secret Hayes was still thrashing in his bed at night over that one.

But along with the exclamation points were question marks. The biggest one was knees. So many had been torn up during 1972 that Ohio State surgeons performed thirteen operations. No other team, college or professional, had spent as much time with its knees on the operating table.

The most famous victim, All-American linebacker Randy Gradishar, had been felled by a torn cartilage in the Indiana game. He missed the following two games, returned to finish the season in spectacular style, but five days after the Rose Bowl was forced to undergo surgery. Then there was Vic Koegel, the outstanding middle linebacker who had missed all but eighty minutes of playing time after being cut down in the Illinois game. And others: defensive ends Tom Marendt and Jim Cope; offensive tackles Scott Dannelley and Tom Swank; linebacker Rocco Rich. Were they completely recovered? Would they be able to regain the full measure of their special gifts, speed and quickness? If the Machine was going to collapse in 1973, it looked as though it would break first at the knees. No wonder Woody Hayes was cutting down scrimmages and contact work, was "sure not going to take any more chances."

Another cloud hung over the Machine as the season began: drugs. The previous spring junior Larry Wiggins, an expected starter at offensive guard, had been busted for selling marijuana and amphetamines. Coach Hayes detests the drug culture and does not even differentiate between a pot-smoking adolescent and a crime-bent heroin addict. So when Wiggins came to his office, asking for help with his defense, seeking a second chance, Hayes stared at him coldly and said no. Wiggins reacted with the assertion that his clientele included players on the team, some of them starters, and threatened to identify them to police. Hayes pounded his fist and called Wiggins a liar, but he was badly shaken. Later when private reports persistently backed up Wiggins's claim, Hayes again lost his temper—at first pledging in front of aides to throw out the offenders, whoever they were, but, finally, deciding to do nothing, which surprised no one. It had been easy enough to dump Wiggins, a single troublemaker who had affronted his personal moral standards. But to drop a whole group of players, to dismember the team, to put his aversion to drugs above the Machine—that was something else.

MULLINS: *Coach, why don't we run down your offensive starters for the coming season. Let's start with the backfield. I guess the fullback would be Champ Henson.*

HAYES: *Yes, certainly nobody is challenging Champ very closely now. There is a freshman putting a little heat on him, which is always good, of course. And Arch Griffin at tailback is still the best tailback. I don't think there is any question but that he and Champ are better than they were a year ago, because they've had a lot of experience and they're both better football players. Fortunately, behind Arch, we have plenty of other good backs. Elmer Lippert has done a good consistent job. He got hurt a little bit in our scrimmage today—he's the only one who did. But we have another young fellow who's coming along very, very well—our other tailback from Washington, D.C.—the name sort of escapes me tonight . . . oh, shoot, I'll get it right now . . . Woodrow Roach. I should be able to get that name, shouldn't I? Well, anyhow, Archie's got some good backup people. But we don't need to worry too much about replacing him unless he gets injured. Archie's a superb football player.*

MULLINS: *How does Baschnagel figure into the situation?*

HAYES: *Well, he figures to be that starting wingback. You know as a freshman, he started three games there. And Brian . . . we have a problem with him, and I mean this seriously. I've never seen a football player work as hard as he does! He works too hard and we're going to have to make him quit next week in order to get an edge on him. He comes out thirty minutes before practice, he catches punts, he catches kickoffs and then he goes over and runs his pass cuts. Then he practices the entire practice. And then he stays there and holds for our extra-point men for another twenty or twenty-five minutes. He's out there too long. I've never seen a kid work as consistently as he does. I've just never seen one!*

MULLINS: *Well, there's another one who works very hard. He anchors the line at offensive tackle—John Hicks.*

HAYES: *Yeah, John works the same way. We've had to ease up on him a couple of days since he's got a little ouchy knee. But John works the same way with the same kind of enthusiasm and a more vocal enthusiasm, too. He makes an awful lot of noise out there! But he also plays an awful lot of football! We've got a lot of good football players. Over on defense those three linebackers are certainly outstanding. I'll let our defensive coach talk about that a little bit later—Coach George Hill. Now this young fellow who played linebacker last year has been moved to defensive tackle—Arnie Jones—and he's doing an exceptionally good job there. So we think we'll have a pretty good football team.*

They had reported, one hundred fifteen in all, to training camp August 25, ready to work and by the accounts of trainers and team physicians, in top fighting trim. Before going home for the summer, each player gets a detailed workout schedule tailored to the individual but in general emphasizing running and weight lifting. Coach Hayes expects everyone, no matter how lowly his spot on the depth chart, to arrive for fall practice in midseason shape. Training camp is not for conditioning, but for developing the ability to take punishment and the need to inflict it.

Camp was several days old when the hitting began in earnest. There were two daily workouts, one two-hour session in the morning, another in the afternoon. It was the hottest weather anybody could remember and the North Facility artificial turf retained the heat like a griddle, raising temperatures on the field to as much as one hundred fifteen degrees. The sun was so fierce that one afternoon four players collapsed on the field.

With off-the-field duties multiplying in recent years, many head coaches have taken to watching their teams practice from isolated spots in the stands or lordly towers high above the fray, and some have even begun skipping workouts altogether. But not Woody Hayes. He is always in the middle of the action, wearing the familiar black OSU baseball cap and flaming-red T shirt; arms folded, jaw jutting, massive paunch protruding, signaling his renowned displeasure at a bungled play by any and every means, from punching his palm to stomping on his cap to shouting an inspired rebuke such as: "Awright, you goddamned sonsofbitches, let's get fucking with it."

Hayes, of course, is no mean psychologist, and around Columbus there are people who insist that some of his wilder tantrums are premeditated to produce maximum impact. Occasionally before a practice he has been seen using a razor blade to slice the threads of his cap so that when he goes berserk over some error, it will tear apart more menacingly —and easily. Some say that on those days when he rips off his wristwatch and jumps up and down on it, he tends to wear a cheap watch. Still, most of his rages seem real enough.

The angriest outburst of this camp came during a controlled (light-hitting) scrimmage. Pete Johnson, a muscular freshman fullback from Long Island's Long Beach High School, had failed several times in succession to execute a certain block. With each mistake, Hayes, standing behind the offensive huddle, grew more livid, clenching and unclenching his fist faster and faster, shouting, finally, "Fullback, you stupid jackass. You're the biggest goddamned jackass I've ever seen."

Johnson, eighteen years old, stared at the ground while other players shifted uneasily, uncertain of what was coming next. Hayes's voice was the only sound on the sun-scorched practice field. "Block, you dumb sonofabitch," he screamed, marching up to Johnson and swatting him hard on the shoulder pads, driving him backward. "Goddamn you, *block.*"

When Johnson again moved towards the wrong hole on the next play, Hayes erupted into a purple-faced frenzy, biting down hard on the heel of his hand, whirling around in fury, then grabbing his own T shirt at the neck and tearing it to shreds.

Despite such explosions, he was pushing the team much less than was his custom. It was still, by most standards, a punishing camp, but there was no doubt that, compared with previous years, the workouts were less exhausting, the blowups less frequent and the scrimmages less bloody. So, inevitably, the question was raised—had Woody Hayes finally loosened up, begun at last to relax inside? Some went so far as to suggest, behind his back, of course, that he was not as tough.

More likely, the answer lay not with any personal transformation but with the character of the team Hayes was coaching. First, obviously, he was worried about injuries, especially after the outbreak of the previous year, and most injuries take place during these preseason practices when stamina and resistance are not yet up to peak level. Second, last year's team had broken down disastrously in the second half of several games, most notably in the Rose Bowl. There was speculation that they had overtrained, left too much of their energies on the practice field, and reluctantly Hayes had come to agree. Thus his Number 1 obsession of the 1973 season: "fresh legs . . . we're going to ease off so come Saturday we'll have those fresh legs." He said it over and over again throughout the fall. Finally, his 1973 Buckeyes were a relatively known quantity. There were questions, sure. But, for the most part, he did not have to bend them

135

to the breaking point to find out who they were. He knew they were experienced, disciplined and in excellent condition. Had they been green, lazy or soft in any way, he would no doubt have cracked the whip as in days of old. It seemed closer to the truth to conclude that the milder workouts reflected a change not of intensity but of strategy.

In further support of that conclusion, Hayes himself remained as compulsive as ever in his attention to organization and detail. As always, he moved himself and his assistant coaches into Stradley Hall, the dormitory where his players live during preseason workouts. From his room on the ninth floor, he watched and supervised everything, conferring with subordinates, poring over reports, planning meals and mapping out daily schedules from the first wake-up call at 7 A.M. until the last team meeting and lights-out at 10:15 P.M.

Never was a minute wasted. When not practicing, eating or sleeping, the players could usually be found meeting. There was a squad meeting before and after every workout. And in the evening after dinner, there were more meetings in which the players divided into smaller groups by position.

The rigid timetable would continue through the season. In Coach Hayes's system there is never a day off for himself or his organization, not even Sunday. That's the day the players come in for their grades on the previous day's game. By 7:30 Saturday night, Hayes and his assistants are back at work, reviewing films of the game and marking each player's performance on every play with a check or a zero. Sunday night is spent watching films of next week's opponent and drawing up final game plans. Monday begins the grueling part of the work week: coaches' meetings, player conferences, and scrimmages with offensive and defensive starters going up against third-string "scout" units who impersonate the upcoming opponents right down to the colors they wear and the numbers on their backs. Coach Hayes overlooks few details.

Even out of football season the Machine never seems to stop. After the last game an Ohio State player can look forward to a winter exercise program that is voluntary in name only, a five-week spring practice when most positions are decided, and finally, the summer workout schedule that has been specially designed for him. Being a Buckeye is a year-round, day-and-night job. "We earn our scholarships and special treatment," says wingback Morris Bradshaw.

As with everything else, preseason practices followed a precise scenario that was broken down to the minute. They began with a half-hour of rugged stretching and isometric exercises, players working together in pairs. After the loosening-up work, the players split into groups by position for another half-hour of special drills. Then full offensive units ran plays against the defensive units. All this, of course, was typical of college workouts. But there was at least one unusual custom. To help eliminate penalties, a Hayes anathema, two paid referees—in full dress with striped shirts and red flags—were on the field every practice. They called infractions just as they would in a game. And just as *he* would in a game, Woody Hayes sometimes barreled onto the field, shouting his rage at a questionable call.

MULLINS: *Cornelius Greene had a great spring, Coach, and . . .*

HAYES: *He had a good fall, not quite as spectacular as this spring. But he's had a good fall and there is some chance he'll be starting next week because Greg Hare has been out for about a week now with a pulled leg tendon and it seems to bother him when he runs now, even though I gave him a week off.*

137

The competition for starting quarterback between Greg Hare and Cornelius Greene shaped up as the highlight of preseason training. Hare, a gentle and soft spoken senior, had quarterbacked the Buckeyes in 1972 and was well liked by teammates, who had elected him offensive captain. He was endowed with size (6′ 3″, 202 pounds), a strong if not always accurate arm and adequate running ability, but seemed to lack the consistency and authority to lead. This was especially evident on option rollouts where he who hesitates is lost. Hare's indecisiveness, some said, was at least partly the result of his inability to withstand the icy glares and jagged rebuffs of his coach. A succession of fumbles and interceptions in the spring game had not elevated the Maryland youngster in Hayes's esteem.

On the other hand, Greene, a sophomore from a Washington, D.C., slum who was nicknamed "Flam" for his flamboyance, had enjoyed a brilliant spring game, running for 116 yards and two touchdowns, passing for 137 yards and another score. Lean and spindly at 6′ 0″, 168 pounds, Greene did not have the kind of bullish physique that usually impresses Coach Hayes. But as Woody admiringly noted after watching him bounce up quickly from several hard shots, "This kid sure takes a helluva beating." Though his passing reminded no one of Joe Namath, his running ability was beyond question. He was a threat to score every time he got past the line of scrimmage.

In earlier years, Greene would probably not have stood a chance for the job. Columbus whites, many of Southern origin, could still be heard saying "nigger" in public, and the idea of a black man quarterbacking their beloved Buckeyes would have been difficult for some of the home folks to swallow. A black defensive back who played for Hayes in the

138

mid-Sixties recalls: "When I was at OSU, Columbus was a tough place for blacks and I don't think Woody could have started a black kid at quarterback. Woody has always been out front of most coaches on racial things. He was the first in the Big Ten to appoint a black assistant. But quarterback is another thing entirely. He's the leader on the field, the object of all eyes. Ohio State was one of the last Big Ten schools to have a black quarterback, and I think some of that had to do with public pressure."

Columbus was still no racial paradise in 1973, but there were blacks on the police force, blacks in the insurance industry, even blacks on the City Council—so why not at quarterback?

A second obstacle for Greene, had he come along sooner, would have been Hayes himself and the notion he held for so long that "You lose one game for every sophomore you start." But of late Woody had become a believer in youth, thanks largely to Rex Kern and his 1968 sophomore-laden "Kiddie Korps." They had showed Hayes how far a team can go with the enthusiasm and confidence that stem from the optimism of inexperience. The nineteen-year-old Greene would fit in nicely with Griffin and Baschnagel, also nineteen-year-old sophomores, and Henson, a twenty-year-old junior. Regardless of Hare's health, it looked as though the Machine would be starting its first black quarterback.

MULLINS: *For the first practice sessions before the pads you ran through a lot of timing and passing drills. Will we see a lot of passing this fall?*

HAYES: *Oh, I hope not too much. I'd like to see better passing. You know, we're always working on the efficiency. Incidentally, this summer, I found a very interesting thing. You want to hear about it?*

139

MULLINS: *Uh-huh.*

HAYES: *Well, we made a study of what wins in football. Actually one of the graduate assistants made the study—Bill Davies is who it was—and he found that the team that ran the most, the team that had the most yardage in running, won about eighty-five percent of the games in the Big Ten. The team that passed the most—it was something down around fifteen percent. And it's just amazing how that running game does stand out in football. Yes, the passing game is definitely subservient to the running game.*

MULLINS: *Coach, you added something new this year. You came in with short dashes instead of long, traditional mile runs. . . .*

HAYES: *Yes, we used to require that each player run a mile in under six minutes the first day of fall practice to see whether he was in shape. Well, we cut out the mile because we think this is better—we know it's better! I don't want to go into intricate detail but we time each man in eight forty-yard sprints. Then we rest him five minutes. Then we time him in eight thirty-yard sprints. Well, if his time stays almost consistent across the board as it did for Brian or Arch, it means they're in almost perfect shape. If they run, say, their fifth sprint and the time starts going up it means they're out of shape. And it was amazing how many players we had who ran their times consistently. As a matter of fact, I gave each player a reward if he did. You know what the reward was? . . . Come on now, you're not trying to guess.*

MULLINS: *Can you tell us what the reward was?*

HAYES: *Yes, I gave them an autographed copy of my book, which I hope they read. And if he ran his time . . . we had about thirty-five fellows on the squad do it . . . about forty I think it was. But we felt they deserved some reward. I don't*

140

know whether they consider it a reward or not.

MULLINS: *You have a copy of that here?*

HAYES: *Oh, I do have but let's not be such . . . let's not get indulged in . . . let's call it crass sports commercialism.*

MULLINS: *It's on sale in Columbus now, isn't it?*

HAYES: *Yeah, you can buy it at any good bookstore. And it's the story of all our players who played so well for us over the years . . . and some of them have gone on to play pro ball . . . and by the time you get all of the players in there you have about seventy chapters right there. . . . A lot of great games and a lot of great players.*

You Win With People! was the title he gave it. He had written it, he said, to counter all the "negative" literature in the bookstores on sports. He was going to tell people what was *right* about college football, and wasn't it about time the true football believer had a book? The result was a hygienic remembrance of things past, a book that stood in relation to its author as a bowl of jello does to nitroglycerine.

Conspicuous in its absence was any commentary on some of the more renowned episodes of his career, events which have made his name synonymous with the words *temper tantrum.* The famous incident at Ann Arbor in 1971—when he roared out on the field claiming a Michigan interception should have been ruled interference, then tore up the sideline down markers—was dismissed in the book with: "On third and 16 from the Ohio 49, the officials ruled that the Michigan safetyman intercepted the pass intended for Dick Wakefield. However, the pictures show unquestionably there was pass interference on this play. The final score was Michigan—10, Ohio State—7." He has told intimates that the referees were "a bunch of crooks," but you won't find him saying that in *You Win With People!*

The book does not even mention what was probably his next most celebrated explosion, just before the 1973 Rose Bowl game. He had become enraged at a pesky Los Angeles *Times* photographer named Art Rogers, who was snapping close-ups of him as he huddled with assistants. Without warning, Hayes charged at Rogers, shoving the camera into his face and bowling him over. The photographer, who suffered from double vision and swollen eyes for several weeks thereafter, pressed charges, and it looked as though Hayes was going to have to go to court. But a few months later Rogers agreed to drop the charges in exchange for a letter of apology from his attacker. In the letter, Coach Hayes was more than conciliatory, saying, "I can see why a good photographer would be almost as eager to get good pictures as a coach is to win a football game, and I am sorry that our intentions came into conflict; for photographic display is certainly an integral part of our game of football." Meanwhile he continued to believe he had been set up, the target of a conspiracy of West Coast newsmen.

Because his mistrust of photographers and reporters extends to editors and publishers, Hayes himself financed the publishing, distribution and advertising of *You Win With People!*, just as he had done with two prior literary ventures. It cost him thirty-five thousand dollars to get the new book out, but at least he didn't have to worry about its being in the hands of some big publisher who would change it around and twist everything.

MULLINS: *One more question before we break for a commercial. What's in store for the Buckeyes this week as they prepare against Minnesota?*

HAYES: *Well, we're going to ease up on our hard work, ease up very much so we can go into this game with fresh legs. We had a pretty good scrimmage today. After I studied the pictures tonight, I saw it was better than I thought it was. But we've got to be sharper both offensively and defensively and I'm sure we can do. We're going to be much, much better than we were this weekend.*

When the camera returns from a commercial, Hayes is flanked by two young men wearing jackets and ties, standing stiffly at attention and looking grim. They are two of the Buckeye captains, the aforementioned Hare, and senior linebacker Rick Middleton. Middleton has grown a bushy goatee and mustache over the summer, and except for his gray letter jacket, he projects the slightly bedraggled image of a modern youth. That Coach Hayes permits some freedom of appearance comes as a surprise to many people. These people do not understand what the Machine means to Woody Hayes. While Woody may not like deep sideburns, Afros, beards, mustaches, high-heeled shoes and wing collars, he is politically astute enough to avoid taking positions he cannot defend, forcing confrontations that would only damage the Machine. As he says, "We control by attitudes not by rules."

Just as Hayes has learned, for the sake of the Machine, to live with new dress styles, so has he learned to back down when enough of his players stand up and challenge him.

During the 1972 season Hayes became angered at the occasional tardiness of an offensive lineman, Chuck Bonica, probably the strongest member of the team. One afternoon Bonica arrived five minutes late for practice and discovered he had been suspended from the squad, his locker sealed by a new padlock. When Bonica protested his punishment, Hayes flew into a frenzy, calling him everything he could think of and vowing he was finished with football at Ohio State. Later at a team meeting, the coach continued his ranting, "Who in the hell does he think he is? Who is he to come in late all the time?"

It went on until cocaptain George Hasenohrl, an All-American defensive tackle highly respected by his teammates, stepped forward to denounce the harsh punishment and threatened a walkout by the entire team unless Bonica were reinstated. As he talked, other players nodded their support of the defiance, while the assistant coaches looked on, waiting for Coach Hayes to blow.

But when Hasenohrl finished, Hayes, in an astonishingly gentle voice, praised him and his teammates for their show of independence, saying, "I sure admire you fellas for standing up for what you think is right. That takes guts." The assistant coaches joined in with their approval, as Hayes ordered Bonica's locker reopened.

HAYES: *We'll start tonight with our cocaptains, Rick Middleton, our defensive captain, and Greg Hare, our offensive captain. Let's see just how they do approach this season which is their last. What can you say about that, Rick?*

MIDDLETON: *Well, as for being a senior and being a captain, everyone wants to end up their career with the best season ever, and I think as a defensive captain we feel we're set up to be one of the best defensive squads ever.*

HAYES: *Why do you say that now?*

MIDDLETON: *Well, I think we got the talent, and I think it's just a matter of putting the desire into everybody there.*

HAYES: *How do you put desire in?*

MIDDLETON: *It's just a matter of pride.*

HAYES: *Now, what do you mean by* pride? *Come on now, you can tell me.*

MIDDLETON: *Pride is something you want to instill in every-*

body. One of the things that Coach Hill told us earlier in the year is that there's never been a team at Ohio State that's gone undefeated that hasn't been a national champion. So if we win them all, we got it locked up.

HAYES (chuckling): *Well, that's all we'll take. Greg, you've been bothered today with this bad knee. Now, when did you get that . . . when did you first notice it?*

HARE: *Well, I've had this injury for around two years. It just comes on and off.*

HAYES: *When did you first notice it?*

HARE: *The first time was before the Northwestern game my sophomore year. I pulled a tendon behind my knee . . . and it's just given me a lot of trouble and then it goes away. I don't think it's anything to really worry about. It just takes time. . . .*

HAYES: *It's kept you out of about a week's work, and a fella's bound to miss some sharpness if that happens.*

HARE: *That's true, because I felt it today when I went in. I didn't have all the timing that I had . . .*

HAYES: *That's right, it was noticeable in there. Yeah, it was noticeable and that week's work does mean a lot. So we got to get you back and going on Monday even though you're a little bit gimpy. You know these injuries are funny. The second time you get them they hurt, but they're never as bad as they are at first. Now don't ask me why, but you'll find that it won't bother you as much. You can live with it better the second time around than the first. . . . I don't know. Maybe it's just a matter of compensation and getting used to it. Does it bother your passing?*

HARE: *No, I think—*

HAYES: *Which leg is it in?*

HARE: *It's my right leg, but it really doesn't bother my passing too much. It's just that quick acceleration and sprinting that it hurts mostly.*

HAYES: *Yeah, I think you're right. I thought you had the ball on target pretty well today. And, of course, you've developed a better arm this year than you had a year ago, so you'll just have to live with it and go from there, won't you?*

HARE: *Yes, sir.*

HAYES: *Okay, men, we got some other people to show so I'm going to cut you sort of short tonight. Thanks for coming down, okay?*

HARE:
MIDDLETON: } *Okay.*

Next Hayes is joined by a trio of his best athletes: Randy Gradishar, John Hicks and Harold "Champ" Henson. As with Hare and Middleton, they are lined up like wooden statues, their faces tight and solemn.

Gradishar is the chief bone-crusher of a defense whose *modus operandi* is to hit anything that moves. An unsmiling, baby-faced twenty-two-year-old from Champion, Ohio, he is a ball hawk who prowls around the OSU defense as Woody does the sideline. He will go into the left side, the right side, cheat to the middle, pick up a receiver, move to the line for a blitz, and rarely does he make a mistake. There are a lot of brutal tacklers on the defense, but Gradishar seems to make his victims bounce higher and stay down longer. If his knee troubles can be put behind him, Buckeye coaches believe he will enter the pros as the best linebacker from the Big Ten since Dick Butkus.

Right tackle John Hicks, like Gradishar, is another fierce individual with a history of knee problems. He missed the entire 1971 season after surgery but recovered enough the next year to be unanimously voted an All-American. When Woody Hayes speaks of his players, the name that comes up most often is John Hicks. Hicks is a devastating blocker, a 6'3", 258-pound black senior who takes off from the line of scrimmage at a full gallop. And Hayes, never one to overlook the contributions of the big tackle who opens the holes, calls Hicks "the greatest lineman I've ever had."

Hayes's adoration for Hicks goes far deeper than football ability. John Hicks is Woody Hayes's idea of what a young man should be—rah-rah, straight-arrow and clean-cut. Hicks belongs to the Fellowship of Christian Athletes, addresses Hayes as *sir,* and is not averse to keeping his coach abreast of developments in other players' private lives. In a world where not every college football player seems to have these virtues anymore, Woody Hayes delights in John Hicks. To show his appreciation, Hayes appointed Hicks cocaptain of the team after the players, via the ballot box, had chosen Middleton and Hare. It struck some as a peculiar version of democracy and disturbed a number of black players who regarded Hicks as "Woody's boy." But Hayes didn't care. John Hicks is Woody Hayes's favorite Buckeye.

Only a notch or two lower in Buckeye affection is Harold Henson, whose father nicknamed him "Champ" when he was just a shade bigger than a football. Henson is the archetypal Ohio State fullback, squarely in the bruising workhorse tradition of Bob White, Bob Ferguson, Jim Otis and John Brockington. He has a sweet farmboy face, looks bigger than his listed 6'4", 228 pounds, and hits the line each time as if he were trying to make a first down against the Chicago Police Department. The year before he had butted his way relentlessly into the heart of Woody Hayes and across opponents' goal lines on twenty occasions to lead the nation in touchdowns. With Henson there is no fakery, no sharp cuts or dancing feet; it is all straight-ahead, crunching, cement-block power. Champ Henson plays what Woody Hayes calls FOOTBALL.

MULLINS: *Champ, before Coach starts in with his questions, I want to give you something. This is the official Street and Smith College Football Yearbook and your picture is on the front page.*

HAYES: *Doesn't he look mean?*

MULLINS: *This is a special leather-bound edition for you, Champ.*

HENSON: *Thank you very much.*

MULLINS: *Okay, Coach.*

HAYES: *Okay, Ted, I think I know what Champ will do with that. He'll probably take it home and give it to his dad, and his dad will be more prideful about it than Champ is, because Champ's got new challenges to think about this year. The fact that he led the nation in touchdowns last year means there'll be a lot of people trying to stop him this year. Don't forget that, Champ.*

HENSON: *I won't.*

HAYES: *It hasn't made you big-headed, has it?*

HENSON: *I hope not.*

HAYES: *What do you think of these two All-Americans standing next to you, Randy Gradishar and John Hicks? Has it made them big-headed?*

HENSON: *I don't think so.*

HAYES: *I don't think it has, either. I don't know of two men who could bask in their glory and do it without it bothering them more than John Hicks and Randy Gradishar, and from the shape they came back in . . . Randy, let's talk just for a minute about these tests you underwent—and incidentally he*

148

went through them real well. *What do you think of them as compared to the mile?*

GRADISHAR: *Well, I think it's a lot better conditioning and—*

HAYES: *Why?*

GRADISHAR: *Well before, we had to do the mile, and as you find out, you really don't play football running a mile. You play it running sprints, and I think if you condition for sprints you're better off in the long run in the game.*

HAYES: *Now you were starting on sort of a new knee. Did it bother you—the sprinting on the knee?*

GRADISHAR: *Well, I had some work in the sprints. I didn't have any contact but I did work a lot on the weights and running. And this summer when I did work out I worked out without my brace, and it felt real good. I'm just wearing my brace now for a safety precaution.*

HAYES: *Has it bothered you at all?*

GRADISHAR: *It's been a little bit sore. But the doctor said it's going to be sore just from the normal playing football so I'll have to live with it, I guess.*

HAYES: *I guess you will. That's right . . . Umm-hm . . . John had a knee injury a couple of years ago but it doesn't bother you now, does it?*

HICKS: *No, sir.*

HAYES: *Could you tell us which one it is? I wouldn't even know from the way you play football.*

HICKS: *It's the left one, sir.*

HAYES: *It's the left one. Well, it's nice to know but I don't think it's going to bother you any. John, you're in your fifth year of college football, aren't you?*

HICKS: *Yes, sir.*

HAYES: *You see, John was hurt in preseason practice before*

149

his junior year started, so he was awarded another year of eligibility. *And how do you approach this, your fifth year? How do you keep from getting bored in playing football this long in college?*

HICKS: *Well, you know it's a lot of fun, a lot of hard work, but it's something you like to do . . . it's something I like to do, sir.*

HAYES: *I know you do and you play it with great enthusiasm, and you don't get to see this other fellow play much or practice much, but they tell me Randy plays about the same way.*

HICKS: *Yes, sir.*

HAYES: *Umm-hm . . . What new challenges would you have this year now, over last year?*

HICKS: *Well, I've looked at a lot of films from last year, sir. I think I can do a lot of things better this year. . . . I just want to do everything better. You know, I hope that the team . . . well, I know when we put it together we can win the title and that's the thing I want to do more than anything.*

HAYES: *You feel tired now?*

HICKS: *Yes, sir, we had a scrimmage today and I'm pretty tired.*

HAYES: *I kind of thought that. Now we only went three quarters today and next week you'll have to go four quarters. Randy, how tired are you now?*

GRADISHAR: *I feel pretty good now. I thought my knee was going to be sore after today's scrimmage. It really felt good and my legs feel good and I'll be ready for next week.*

HAYES: *Now we kept that Astroturf wet today. Do you think that helps your knee?*

GRADISHAR: *Well, personally, I don't like the field real wet.*

150

I like it a little bit damp because it doesn't grab as much when it's dry.

HAYES: *You mean it doesn't grab as much when it's wet as when it's dry, don't you?*

GRADISHAR: *Yeah, that's right.*

HAYES: *But you like it a little damp, huh?*

GRADISHAR: *Yeah, that's right.*

HAYES: *You know when we start out with it a little damp, by the end of the practice it's totally dry and it starts grabbing, and then you get sore knees and even sore hamstrings. Champ, how do you like the field right now? How do your knees feel now?*

HENSON: *Pretty good, I guess.*

HAYES: *What do you mean, "pretty good"?*

HENSON: *Uh . . . real good. Real good!*

HAYES: Well now do they or don't they?

HENSON: *They feel good. I'm surprised.*

HAYES: *Now what are you surprised about? I'll tell you something I'm surprised about. Can you guess?*

HENSON: *No.*

HAYES: *I've been going over your films. Now what do you think I'm surprised about?*

HENSON: *I don't know.*

HAYES: *Now come on, you should know the answer. It's your blocking. Your blocking is getting a lot better. It's not perfect yet. But I know when you were in high school all you did was carry the football and you never learned how to block. Well you're getting better at it. Now I don't mean it doesn't need a little more work, but you're definitely getting better. You've got the feel of it now—it's coming to you. And it isn't easy to learn to be a good blocker, particularly when you're spending an awful lot of time carrying the ball. But on the other hand when you stop to realize how many people block for you, you can spend some time doing it, too. And you're getting better. Arch will be happy about that, too. And Arch had a pretty good day, didn't he?*

HENSON: *Yes, sir.*

HAYES: *Yeah, he runs pretty well . . . Umm-hm. Umm-hm . . . Well, John, what else have you got to tell us now? Have you got a few words of wisdom for this season?*

HICKS: *No, sir.*

HAYES: *You don't have, huh? Except you're going to win them all?*

HICKS: *Yes, sir.*

HAYES: *Okay, Randy Gradishar. What can you add to that?*

GRADISHAR: *Well, not really too much. I just think that if we go out and play the best we can all season and get together as a team, with our talent, we should win it all.*

HAYES: *Yes, we should.*

GRADISHAR: *Yes, sir.*

HAYES: *Champ, you're going to be better this year?*

HENSON: *Yes, sir.*

HAYES: *Okay, all right . . . I'll be depending on all three of you, and the public has heard you make your announcements so now you've got to live up to it. Thanks for being on the show, fellas. Thanks very much.*

The players leave and into the picture steps George Hill, head of the defensive unit. A large, pear-shaped man, the thirty-seven-year-old Hill is like every other assistant coach in the business: he aspires to be head coach. As defensive coordinator and number one assistant, he is the heir apparent to Woody Hayes's seat, but he had better be a patient man.

152

Hill idolizes Hayes and it shows in his speech patterns, which bear a striking resemblance to his boss's, right down to the last "umm-hm." An interview one day with Hill quickly turned into an encomium, with the assistant coach gushing admiration of Hayes's rule. "I want to say something about my boss . . . he is the greatest coach . . . the greatest *man* . . . in the whole goddamned world . . . umm-hm . . . umm-hm. . . ."

MULLINS: *This is the defensive coordinator of the Ohio State Buckeyes, George Hill, and Woody, I get to interview him. George, I'd like to start off with finding out about Arnie Jones, the man who did such a tremendous job last year at middle linebacker when Vic Koegel got hurt. This year he's been switched to tackle, right?*

HILL: *Right, Ted. Arnie had an outstanding year, we felt. He came along and got stronger each ball game last season, and at the end of the season he was an excellent football player for us. As we prepared for the season, there just wasn't any way we could leave him or Vic Koegel sitting on the bench, and we felt we had to find some other place for one of them. We felt that Arnie played the down alignment just a little bit better than Vic, and Vic might have been just a little bit better pass defender than Arnie. So we moved Arnie to defensive tackle. He's a quick learner and he picked the thing up real well, and I just viewed the films here a little bit ago myself and Arnie had an excellent scrimmage. He's strong, he's quick and I'll tell you one thing—those big tackles are going to have trouble getting into him.*

MULLINS: *Were you worried about his size? He's what, about two hundred ten pounds?*

HILL: *No, I don't worry about size. I worry about speed and quickness and how hard they hit people.*

MULLINS: *Why don't you run down the starting defense for us right now, as if the season were starting tonight.*

HILL: *Well, on the open side end we have a returning letterman who we think is one of the fine defensive ends in the country; Van DeCree had an excellent season as a sophomore. Van's quick and he's got great athletic ability, and Van played really ten excellent football games for us last football season, and we think a lot of him. At our right tackle we have another returning man, Pete Cusick, who is probably the strongest man on our football team, and Pete has started off the fall where he left off last year, and we think he's going to be an excellent tackle for us. Our open side linebacker is, of course, Randy Gradishar, who is returning as a third-year starter for us, and we've already talked about Randy here. We think he's an excellent football player. Vic Koegel's coming back off that injury last season and we think the world of him. As a sophomore he was really the core of our defense, and it shook us up when we lost him. Our captain, Rick Middleton, is our boundary side linebacker and had an outstanding season for us last year, and we're expecting a great deal of leadership and linebacking from Rick this year. At our other tackle, of course, is Arnie Jones, and our boundary side end right now would be Jim Cope. Now Jim was a backup to Tom Marendt last year, and when Marendt got hurt early in the season, Jimmy started the rest of the season. Right now Jim's our starter and it's going to be a couple of weeks before Tom Marendt is quite ready to play, but I'll tell you—he's a competitor, and he's going to get back in there as soon as he can. In our secondary we have Neal Colzie at our open side halfback. He'll be a junior this year. He had an excellent spring and has started off this year doing an outstanding job, Ted. His interception today was a real peach: he went back on a long pass and got up in the air, and he really went after the football, which is what a defensive back has to do. Our safety will be Rich Parsons, our cornerback will be Timmy Fox and our boundary side halfback will be Steve Luke. All these people are young and have gotten much, much stronger all fall. So we've got football players that are pretty darned good and we've got some people backing them up who are going to push them. And I think this is what a fine football team is—when you've got that kind of competition.*

MULLINS: *A lot of experience and depth. And we have time now to mention one more time the* You Win With People! *book that came out two weeks ago and is now on sale at all the stores here in Columbus, and it makes excellent reading. I read it for myself and it's very easy to read. A lot of names you'll remember back through Ohio State history under Coach Woody Hayes. Woody, a couple of comments now about the first game against Minnesota.*

HAYES: *Well, we think this will be the toughest opener we've ever, ever had! They had a fine team when they came here last year and from all the reports, they've picked up a lot of junior college players who they figure on stepping in right away, and they have enormous speed, both on the offense and defense, and we know they had a fine offense last year. It led the league in running, and we expect they'll try to start off the same way, and our job is certainly cut out for us. It won't be easy at all.* It will be one of the hardest football games we've ever played!

MULLINS: *So the first game of the season will be next Saturday afternoon in Ohio Stadium against the Golden Gophers of Minnesota. We hope you'll join Woody next Saturday evening here on Channel Ten. Woody, thank you.*

HAYES: *Thank you, and good night, fans.*

155

The older you get the more legal you get.

He had made the decision. The Machine was not just going to beat the Minnesota Gophers in its opening game. It was going to humble them. He was in a vengeful frame of mind and there would be no mercy.

Woody Hayes's dark mood could be traced to the Minnesota coach, Cal Stoll. Hayes had little use for Stoll. For one thing, Stoll had replaced Woody's long-time friend, Murray Warmath, as Minnesota head coach. But there was more to it than just friendship and loyalty. What really infuriated Hayes was Stoll's recruiting.

In only a year Stoll had scored a remarkable series of

recruiting triumphs. A superb salesman, good-looking, energetic and youthfully mature, Stoll could boast of assembling the Big Ten's best group of 1973 freshmen. With the help of a hustling staff and rejuvenated booster organizations, he landed one of the country's most pursued blue-chippers, a junior college transfer named Rick Upchurch. That alone would have been an impressive coup, but Stoll quickly surpassed it by reaching into the state of Michigan—a first for a Minnesota coach—and snatching no fewer than eight prized prospects. With Stoll grabbing players from Michigan, Wolverine recruiters began invading Ohio with greater force, challenging the Machine on its own turf. Woody Hayes was not happy.

The subject of Minnesota's recruiting came up one morning while I was visiting Hayes in his St. John Arena office a couple of months before the 1973 opener. He had been talking casually of a former Ohio State *Lantern* reporter who had gotten a job on the sports desk of the Minneapolis *Tribune*. He noted that the young writer had a taste for investigative reporting.

"Where he's going, he may find something to write about," Hayes said grimly, running his fingers through his ash-white hair.

"Why?" I asked. "Is something going on up there?"

Hayes leaned back in his chair. He was sitting under a photograph of himself with John Glenn. The office walls were covered with photographs of colonels, admirals and generals. In the picture with Glenn, Hayes's face was aglow with a big gap-toothed smile. He was not smiling now.

"The word gets around pretty fast when you're pulling cute ones," he said after a pause. He leaned forward. "Our tip-off on this thing was that some of the kids we were trying to recruit didn't even want to visit our campus. They just shook their heads and said 'no thank you.' Now that's pretty goddamned unusual."

What was not unusual was the response to Stoll's recruiting success. It is almost a law of college football that when a new coach arrives on the scene and signs a few too many attractive prospects, threatening the status quo, the other coaches, particularly those on top, grow resentful and often skeptical. Complaints are privately voiced, gossip spread, accusations whispered. Stoll had set in motion the Big Ten rumor mill, there was no dispute about that. And whether the grist was real or not, Woody Hayes and some other people around the Big Ten were almost inevitably going to speculate that Minnesota might be offering improper inducements.

Upchurch, of course, was the conversation centerpiece, partly because junior college transfers are rarities in Big Ten athletics. A speedy black halfback from the Toledo area, Upchurch had been heavily recruited in high school, but his grades were too low to qualify him for a four-year college. At Indian Hills Community College in Centerville, Iowa, Upchurch's academic average improved almost as much as his rushing average, which is usually what happens to athletes at junior colleges. Once again the recruiting hunt for his services was on, with Iowa apparently leading the chase. Some figured Nebraska might come on strong, and Ohio State still had a chance, but not Minnesota. Minnesota seemed to be nowhere in the running.

From Minnesota's point of view, it could be argued that the successful sales pitch to Upchurch, as well as to the other flashy prospects, had been spotlessly clean. In recruiting, a coach looks for any rhetorical edge he can find, and Stoll's

158

defenders reasoned that Upchurch had been won over by some weighty arguments: first, Minnesota had always been a comfortable place for black athletes; second, at Minnesota Upchurch would be an immediate starter, a claim which could not be made by Nebraska or Ohio State; and finally, Minneapolis had a hell of a lot more going for it than Iowa City. As for Stoll's recruiting conquests in Michigan—which reportedly had agitated Michigan coach Bo Schembechler to the point of saying, "I want to beat Minnesota bad when we play them this year, real bad"—there was nothing really astonishing there. Stoll had served as an assistant under Duffy Daugherty at Michigan State for eleven years, so his roots in the state were deep, his contacts extensive.

There seemed to be good logical answers to all the questions. But the rumors persisted anyway, fed in part by what everyone knew about the Minnesota athletic department's financial woes. After an era of winning and self-sufficiency in the early and mid-Sixties, the school had fallen into the bad habit of fielding weak football teams. As losses on the field piled up, so did those at the box office, and the growing popularity of the professional team in town, the Minnesota Vikings, did not help. It was common to see half of Memorial Stadium's fifty-six thousand seats empty at kickoff time. By 1973, the Minnesota athletic department had dropped $500,-000 into red ink, and officials were predicting a deficit of $800,000 in the next three years.

"They saw they were dying and maybe they got a little desperate," Woody Hayes said in his office.

"If you think something is going on," I said, "why not do something about it?"

"What *can* I do about it?" he shot back.

"Report it to the Big Ten commissioner's office. Call a

press conference. Make the accusations out in the open. Hold up your evidence and . . ."

"Naw, naw," he interrupted, his voice growing louder now. "I couldn't do any of that."

"Why not?"

Hayes cracked his fist down on the desk. "Goddamnit, there's enough of you writers going around tearing down the game of football without Woody Hayes standing up and yelling about cheating. I'll be a sonofabitch if I'm going to add to all the negative stuff that's being said about the game."

"What about reporting it to the commissioner?"

Hayes let out a sigh. "Now, that's no good either. Then the other coaches would think I was trying to run things. Y'see, the thing is, I'm not interested in exposing people and taking away their jobs. I just want to bring people into compliance with the rules. That's all. Bring them into compliance.

"About ten years ago we had a similar situation," Hayes went on. "One of our Big Ten coaches went to the commissioner's office and told him the Indiana coach, Phil Dickens, was cheating. So the commissioner—at the time it was Tug Wilson—suspends Dickens and the school gives him the sack. Now that just wasn't right, and I blame the commissioner. What he should've done is call Dickens in and given him a warning. I don't like to see a coach thrown out on his ass like that. Now the irony of the thing is that this other coach, the guy who ratted, wasn't too straight himself. I had six violations against him, six players who'd been gotten illegally. So I went to Wilson and I told him this coach was doing the same things. 'Where's your proof?' he says to me. And I say, 'I'll show you six cases if you bring this coach into compliance, but I won't show you if you're going to suspend him.' So Wilson hemmed and hawed for a while, but finally agreed to accept the evidence on that basis. To this day this coach has hated my guts because he thought I ratted on him. But he didn't realize what a favor I'd done him. He was a fine coach. He just cut corners."

"How much corner-cutting is there in college football?" I asked.

"Oh," he answered pensively, "it's . . . it's cleaner than most people think. Most of us don't cheat. I can tell you *we* don't cheat. I don't know if you believe that, but we don't. Now you take a fella like my good buddy, Bear Bryant. When Bear was at Texas A&M a while back, I understand he was crooked as a dog's hind leg. Awww, there wasn't any doubt about it. He was pulling some cute ones. They tell me Bear is just as straight as a string now. It seems to be the rule in this profession: The older you get the more legal you get."

Woody Hayes had suffered through his own scandal in his early years at Ohio State, because of the personal loan fund he had set up for his players. Was the rule true in his case?

"Yes, I think so," came the reply, delivered more matter-of-factly than might have been expected. "Y' see, the older you get, the more you see that the rules are just about the only thing holding up this society. These days, post-Vietnam, what worries me is that everyone has decided to live up to his own rules."

Is Woody Hayes capable of breaking the rules? Coaches who have recruited against him appear to agree that he is as straight as anybody in the business. They say the Machine is clean because it doesn't have to be dirty. "He's an ethical coach," says Duffy Daugherty, formerly of Michigan State. "His recruiting organization is unsurpassed. His is the only Big Ten school in his state, and he is in the heart of the best

161

talent area in the country. He works hard, has the reputation and takes the best of the best. He can afford to play by the rules." Says Notre Dame's Ara Parseghian, who served as freshman coach under Hayes at Miami of Ohio: "Woody does a lot of things you might say are unusual in an adult, but I think most people in the business will tell you he is honest." And Minnesota's Cal Stoll himself says, "As far as I know, Woody is completely honest and aboveboard."

But some of Hayes's own players refuse to buy the Lincoln-esque portrayal. They say that bounty is there for certain star athletes who want it, and some do. According to the players, a number of committeemen expect to do minor favors for the boys they've helped recruit, and some are willing to do major favors. One committeeman reportedly made regular deposits for four years in the checking account of an offensive tackle's parents. Another committeeman is said to have sold his two-year-old Cadillac to a Buckeye quarterback for five dollars. A committeeman's generosity can usually keep pace with a player's needs.

For a larger group of Buckeyes, there is the summer job program—traditionally a graceful way to profit from college football and referred to by one committeeman as "the fudge factor." NCAA rules forbid players to work during the school year, except holidays, but allow schools to arrange summer jobs as long as the athlete does the work he is paid for and makes no more money than a nonathlete would. The trouble is, it's not easy to check up on what a boy's job really is, whether he's actually doing it or how much it's worth. That's where the "fudge" comes in.

Several years ago a committeeman in Cleveland arranged to have one of his players, a defensive halfback, work as a lifeguard. Anybody drowning would have been on his own,

162

because the player couldn't swim. But he earned a thousand dollars a month and did not have to tell anyone he was getting paid to play at Ohio State. He was just a hard-working lifeguard.

Not everyone, of course, is on the take. Most Ohio State football players are honest. But, as some of the players themselves say, there are enough generous arrangements, loans and gifts, courtesy of the committeemen, that as head coach Woody Hayes cannot be unaware of them. He knows about them, they say, because it would be impossible not to.

Ralph Holloway, a tackle on the Rex Kern–Jack Tatum teams, who acknowledges having received some small dispensation from his committeeman, sums up Hayes's attitude toward the alleged misdeeds this way: "Personally he is completely strait-laced, never takes a nickel from anybody. When the dealers offer him a free car, he always turns it down. In my opinion Woody, unlike a lot of coaches, is not capable of an outright violation like offering a player cash to come to school. I never heard of that, anyway. But at the same time he *is* capable of turning his back when the alumni do their thing for Ohio State football."

Says Glen Hodge, a defensive halfback who quit the team after repeated run-ins with Hayes: "We had a real racket that I know Woody knew about. Each player would get a bunch of tickets to the games for his family and then he'd be entitled to buy another bunch at cut-rate prices. Well, there was this scalping organization and a lot of the players would sell them the tickets which were supposed to be for their families. I remember we'd get our tickets after lunch and there'd be a mad rush to meet the scalper who'd be carrying around these shoe boxes with nothing but twenty-dollar bills. Sometimes your sponsor would buy some tickets, too. Let me tell you, some of the guys used to make two hundred bucks a game selling those tickets. Woody would just ignore it. I think he rationalized it by telling himself that he isn't part of it and that it's happening at a lot of other places, too. You know, he's probably right on that last count. Everybody cheats a little."

While Hayes disavows any knowledge of such shenanigans, the question is still sometimes raised whether he could put a stop to them if he really wanted to. It would be a disagreeable task. The committeemen are the heart of the Machine, a major source of its recruiting power, and to tamper with the committee would be politically unwise. Besides, the shenanigans have been in college football a lot longer than he has, and while not so common as they once were in his organization or so blatantly conspicuous as in many big-time football programs, they are still in the Machine. As long as they exist in moderation and he does not personally have to involve himself, it seems that Woody Hayes can live with them, just as he can live with long hair. Everybody cheats a little.

But the looking-the-other-way attitude did not extend to the rumored sins of Coach Stoll of Minnesota. In Hayes's mind, Stoll had crossed the line that separates fair from unfair. He would have to be taught a lesson. Not by blowing the whistle. No. Woody Hayes would punish Stoll the way he knew best—on the football field.

In preparation for Minnesota, Hayes ran the Machine as scared as he possibly could. All week long before the game, he talked of his upcoming opponent in lavishly ominous terms, as if they were the Minnesota Vikings, not the Minnesota Gophers. "This is going to be the toughest opener we've *ever, ever* had," he intoned over and over at team meetings. His arguments were persuasive. The previous year the Buckeyes had beaten Minnesota by only eight points, and this would be a bigger, and more significantly, faster Gopher team, with one of the best groups of freshmen in the country. Then there was the addition of the dazzling speedster Upchurch, who, after scoring five touchdowns in his team's spring game, had been awarded the nickname "Black Magic." Alongside Upchurch in the backfield would be John King, a two-hundred-twenty-pound fullback who had led the Big Ten in rushing in 1972. Blocking for them would be a typical Minnesota line: big, rough and experienced. And the defense had plenty of young men who really knew how to hit.

With the accent on how menacing Minnesota was, Hayes deftly forgot to mention that the team had compiled a less than glittering 4–7 record in 1972, that most of its starters were green, that its defense was disorganized and beset by injuries and that the national wire-service polls had completely ignored the Gophers while ranking the Buckeyes third. To hear Hayes tell it, this opponent shaped up as tough as any in the nation, and he seemed to have just about everybody convinced. Everybody perhaps except the Las Vegas oddsmakers, who had sized up the situation and installed Ohio State as a twenty-point favorite.

To dramatize his seriousness, Hayes called an early halt to practice each day, cutting out all tough contact drills. When a reporter wondered about the shortened, relaxed practice sessions, Hayes said, "We're playing a team with enormous speed. We have to make sure we have our fresh legs."

His acute sense of psychology, his gamesmanship, was hard at work. The day before the game, addressing the weekly luncheon of the Agonis Club, a local booster organization, he dug into military lore and came up with a morality tale to illustrate the dangers of taking the enemy too lightly. German Field Marshal Rommel, it seems, decided to take a day off to be with his mistress on her birthday. The date of that indiscretion: June 6, 1944; D-Day, the Allied invasion of Normandy.

"The height of human desire is what wins, whether it's on the Normandy Beach or in Ohio Stadium," Coach Hayes told the boosters. He didn't mention that Rommel's own "height of human desire" is what got him into trouble in the first place. As for his own troops, Hayes reported that there were lots of butterflies floating around in their stomachs, always a good sign. "A horse can't go to the starting gate chewing on his oats."

Later at practice he walked over to the north end of the stadium where the hundred-fifty-piece Ohio State marching band was going through its final preparations. After conducting the band through a couple of choruses of "The Buckeye Battle Cry," he delivered a short pep talk. "Awright, you fellas better be ready tomorrow. We're counting on you, goddamnit." His game face was tightly in place.

The game. It was a warm Indian-summer day with a blue sky. By noon thousands of students were streaming across campus and thousands of cars were swooping in off the interstates, all converging on Ohio Stadium. Their dominant colors and bumper stickers left no doubt about the prevailing sentiment. A fin-tailed Cadillac hearse painted scarlet and gray carried GO BUCKS on its sides and rear. In the parking lots men and women dressed in scarlet and gray raised the trunks of their cars and lifted out folding chairs, tables, picnic baskets and whiskey bottles. Children cavorted with scarlet-and-gray miniature footballs, while their parents

166

played cards and read newspapers whose front pages were scarlet and gray. Inside the stadium the Ohio State marching band, in scarlet-and-gray British Grenadier uniforms, was out on the field, striking up "The Buckeye Battle Cry" with the vigor ordered by Coach Hayes. Cheerleaders, their scarlet-and-gray miniskirts appliquéd with Buckeye leaves, were jumping and strutting about on the sidelines. For all of them the day would end happily only when the bells of Orton Tower rang out, as they do after every Ohio State home victory. The bells are silent when the Buckeyes lose. There have been one hundred twenty-five home games since the Hayes era began, and the bells have been still just twenty-seven times.

At exactly 1:25 the crowd of more than eighty-seven thousand people let out a leonine roar as the Ohio State University football team exploded out of its clubhouse under Orton Tower and galloped across the field, waving arms and fists and screaming like Hollywood Apaches who had just spotted a wagon train. They swarmed together at midfield in a mass of jumping, bumping, grunting muscle. In the middle of the free-for-all, a portly sixty-year-old man in a black baseball cap, white shirt, gray slacks and scarlet-and-gray striped tie loosened at the neck, knew his boys were ready. He had been through it all so many times before.

Minnesota's kicker, Steve Goldberg, teed up the ball. This was it, what, in the end, the Machine was all about. The twenty-third season of Wayne Woodrow Hayes as coach of the Ohio State Buckeyes was under way.

Goldberg's kickoff came down at the 7-yard line, where Archie Griffin fielded it, swung to the left and sprinted down the sideline to the Buckeye 34. Hayes stood in front of the OSU bench, his arm resting on the shoulder of Cornelius

Greene, giving him the first play and delivering last-minute counsel.

The Buckeyes set up in their I formation. Greene took the snap, whirled and tossed a quick pitchout to tailback Griffin who swept right end around a John Hicks block for 4 yards. Then it was Griffin again, this time on a draw over right guard Dick Mack for a pickup of 7 yards and a first down on the OSU 45. On the third play, Greene rolled left on the option, deftly faked a pitch to Griffin and slithered through a hole opened by tackle Kurt Schumacher on the left side for 7 yards. Then it was Champ Henson up the middle for 1 yard and again on the next play for 7. Another first down, now at the Minnesota 40.

It was Woody Hayes's brand of bludgeon football with a vengeance—"grinding meat," as he calls it. Five consecutive running plays, 26 yards and 2 first downs, and along the sidelines Hayes was engineering everything himself, chattering on headsets with assistants upstairs, sending in plays through his split-end messenger service, clapping his hands, yelling encouragement. The season was no more than two minutes old, but already the Machine was running flawlessly.

On the next play, with a first down at the 40, Woody Hayes ordered a pass. Since first-down passes are not usually part of the Hayes game plan, the move stunned just about everyone in the stadium, especially the Minnesota defense. Greene, faking to Henson off tackle, dropped back and threw on target over the middle to a wide-open Brian Baschnagel for 10 yards. Enough basketball. Now it was grinding meat again with Griffin carrying on a quick pitchout for 8 yards and coming back on a draw up the middle for 9 more. It was first and 10 on the Minnesota 13-yard line and Hayes went into his "Robust" offense, which he also refers to, lovingly, as "the old high-buttoned shoe." As the name suggests, the formation is old-fashioned and delivers a kick.

There is nothing subtle about "the old high-buttoned shoe," but then subtlety on the football field has always been regarded by Coach Hayes as a specious virtue. It's a tight-T alignment with three running backs behind the quarterback and the ends pulled in close to the tackles, a "suck-it-up" declaration of purpose, an announcement that a bone-jangling smash into the line is about to take place, a gesture of "try-and-stop-us-if-you-can" contempt.

To add extra blocking, Hayes brought in Doug "Bubba" France, one of the biggest men on the squad at 6' 6", 270 pounds. France delivered immediately with a crunching block that sprung Griffin loose inside left end down to the 2-yard line. Now it was time for Woody Hayes's favorite play: running his fullback right up the rear end of one of his tackles. Hayes calls the play "Patton right" or "Patton left." Henson took the handoff from Greene on a Patton left and banged in over Schumacher, but was stopped a yard short of the goal line. On the next play it was Patton right, Henson behind Hicks and Baschnagel, bulldozing his way in for the score.

The Machine, on its first march of the season, had functioned perfectly. It had been a plodding, relentless drive, as faultless as a Marine precision drill, covering 66 yards in 11 plays, consuming 4 minutes and 32 seconds, demonstrating clearly the lopsided superiority of the Ohio State offense to the Minnesota defense. He was only a touchdown behind, but along the Minnesota sideline, Cal Stoll looked haggard and dispirited, while across the way Woody Hayes had his fist raised in triumph. It was opening day and his Buckeye Machine was at its best.

169

For the Gophers, however, the worst was still to come. Ohio State kicked off and the ball was taken by Upchurch. Dashing to the right side of the field, he collided at his 20-yard line with Ohio State's reserve linebacker Bruce Elia. On his way down Upchurch upchucked the football. The Buckeyes recovered, and Upchurch wobbled toward the OSU bench before a teammate helped him make a midcourse correction. Four plays later, Greene rolled around right end for the score, indulging himself in a modest victory dance before being set upon by teammates. The rout was on.

The Buckeye offense had looked indomitable on its first two series and now it was the defense's turn. Minnesota took over on its own 10-yard line. Fullback King tried the middle and was smacked down hard by middle linebacker Vic Koegel after a gain of one. Then it was King again over the middle for 2 yards before being poleaxed by Koegel and tackle Arnie Jones. On third and 7, Upchurch was sent through on a draw and picked up good but not enough yardage for the first down before being stopped by weak-side linebacker Rick Middleton. Minnesota had held the ball exactly 63 seconds.

After a punt Ohio State took over at its own 40 and began what looked to be another slow, inexorable march toward the goal line. But with third and 9 on the Minnesota 16, Greene's pass in the flat to split end Mike Bartoszek sputtered miserably off target and was intercepted on the dead run by Minnesota's cornerback, Kevin Keller, who appeared to have a wide-open field and a sure touchdown ahead of him. Then Greene showed his speed, as well as some strength, coming all the way across the field and fighting off two blocks to bring Keller down at the Ohio State 38. The wiry quarterback managed to look good even when committing the most grievous of Hayesian sins. But the awakened Minnesota offense moved in for the touchdown in nine plays, narrowing the score to 14–7.

The Gopher comeback was short lived. Griffin, who had already rushed for 79 yards on 10 carries, grabbed the kickoff on the 7, set sail to the left, and behind an architecturally perfect wall of blockers, darted downfield untouched, his red fishnet jersey and gray helmet a blur against the bright green Astroturf. When finally the last Minnesota defender moved in for a clean shot beyond midfield, Griffin planted his foot, feinted a cutback and bolted down the sideline, leaving the would-be tackler in a tangled pileup with himself.

It was a brilliant, breathtaking run that seemed to slice the spirit out of the Gophers and their rooters. One of them, sitting in the press box upstairs, filled the air with obscenities, pounded his fist on the table and picked up his transistor radio, as if to smash it to the ground. The irate fan was not a Minnesota coach or athletic-department staffer but Sid Hartman, sports editor of the Minneapolis *Tribune*.

With Griffin's touchdown, Minnesota came totally unstuck. The Buckeyes managed to cash in even on their own errors. On the last play of the first half, Brian Baschnagel, holding on a field goal attempt, botched the snap from center, picked up the loose ball and dashed madly for the goal line, covering the last 5 yards with a giant, salmon-like plunge over defenders into the end zone.

The second half was academic. Ohio State continued to do everything right and Minnesota everything wrong. The game ended 56–7, proving the Las Vegas oddsmakers better prophets than Coach Hayes, or at least the Coach Hayes of his public utterances. As the bells of Orton Tower rang out, Woody Hayes walked off the field, the game ball jammed into his armpit. There was no traditional postgame handshake with Coach Stoll.

He had given his rival coach a lesson in exactly what the Machine could do, and it was something to gloat over. The Buckeye offense, with starters playing only a little more than a half, had ground out 385 yards and 23 first downs rushing, for an average of more than 6 yards a carry, scoring 5 of the first 7 times they touched the ball. Besides the kickoff return, Griffin had carried 15 times for 129 yards, showing even more speed, elusiveness and knock-down strength than in his freshman season, when he led all OSU rushers. Quarterback Greene, whose playing time as a freshman had been limited to one set of downs, had demonstrated his special attributes of shiftiness and speed on the option rollout, running for 86 yards and a touchdown. Henson, the nation's scoring leader as a sophomore with 20 touchdowns, had picked up where he had left off, hammering the middle for 3 6-pointers. Linemen John Hicks, Jim Kregel, Kurt Schumacher, Dick Mack and Steve Myers had led the runners up the middle and around the corners with power and finesse.

The Buckeye defense had been, if anything, even more dominant. With Koegel plugging up the middle of OSU's 5–2 alignment, Minnesota's King had been held to a mere 51 yards in 17 carries. That had made it easier for the open side of the defense to patrol its area, and end Van DeCree, linebacker Randy Gradishar and cornerback Neal Colzie had limited Upchurch to mostly lateral movement—47 yards on 13 attempts, the longest of them for 6 yards. When the Minnesota quarterbacks tried to pass, the defensive line repeatedly batted down balls and forced hurried throws.

Down in the visitor's clubhouse, Cal Stoll looked like a man who had just learned his disease was terminal. He was leaning against a table in the silent gloom, a paper cup in his hand, his large blue eyes fixed vacantly on the things that had just happened to his team. He talked softly and the words came out very slowly. "They were just . . . too much too soon . . . it was a case of too much green . . . on both sides of the line . . . theirs spelled with an 'e' on the end . . . but they are better . . . much better than a year ago . . . both offensively and defensively . . . Ohio State is a great team . . . they're no longer three yards and a cloud of dust . . . they're twelve yards and a mass of humanity. . . ."

In the winner's locker room, a different epilogue was in progress. The Buckeyes were an exuberant mass of humanity, and Woody Hayes, walking into the room where writers and broadcasters meet with him for official post-mortems, wore a look of vindication. He had made his point. And now he was wrung out, but at peace with himself.

"Has anybody got a Coke for me?" he beamed, plopping down on a wooden bench and stretching his legs. "I'm the winning coach." The stress fell on the word "winning."

"You know, my kids were really nervous before the game," he began paternally. "But they got over it in a hurry. I'd have to say this is the best opener we've ever had. We have to be careful now, though, that we don't get too god-damned complacent."

Somebody handed him a paper cup filled with Coke and he chuckled, "You know, that reminds me of a story about Danny Murtaugh after the Pirates won the World Series one time. I asked Danny what he was going to do to fight complacency the next year. And he looked up at me with that big dumb Irish face and said, 'Woody, if I knew what "complacency" meant, I'd tell you what I was going to do to fight it.' "

The reporters laughed and a team manager came in and slipped him a white piece of paper. "Oh, you've got some stats for me," Woody Hayes grinned, eyes brightening like a little boy's before his birthday cake. He scanned the mimeographed sheet. "Twenty-five first downs—that's not bad. . . . Umm-hm . . . Twenty-three by rushing—that's not bad at all. . . . Umm-hm . . . Now *that's* what I call good football."

Duffy Daugherty once said a tie is just about as thrilling as kissing your sister. Actually it's not nearly that thrilling. It's just a doggone big disappointment.

Other players call him "The Animal," "The Beast." When the Ohio State Buckeyes go on the road, an assistant coach once joked, they ship Champ Henson ahead in a cage.

An inordinate amount of folklore has sprung up already around the short happy-and-unhappy life of Harold Raymond Henson III. It begins with the story of how he got his nickname—how his father, then serving his country in Fort Eustis, Virginia, hitchhiked fifteen hours back to Ohio, eyed his newborn son and proclaimed, "He's got to be a champ." Six months later, according to another story they tell around Columbus, the older Henson, his own football career rudely ended by an appendicitis attack, carried his Champ out to the fifty-yard line of Ohio Stadium and set him down on the sod. "Someday you will punish people on this field," said father to son. "Someday you will be a Buckeye."

The prophecy has been fulfilled. A big and square-jawed junior now at the start of the 1973 season, Champ Henson has already hit and hurt more than his share of people. He has grown up to become the core of the Ohio State offense, the key field agent of the Machine. Champ Henson plays fullback and fullback is the position of Woody Hayes's heart.

Champ Henson's job, as Coach Hayes conceives it, requires that he survive the assaults of a half-dozen tacklers twenty-five to forty-five times a game. This demands indifference to fatigue and pain, perhaps mud, rain or snow, not to mention punching, kicking, gouging, scratching and a hundred other brutalities inspired by Woody Hayes's "three-yards-and-a-cloud-of-dust" offense. Most Saturday afternoons Champ Henson performs his job well.

Now, however, it is not Saturday afternoon but Monday night, and Champ Henson, without shoulder pads, cleats or helmet, is standing in the Formica Modern lobby of his south campus dorm. Tough-guy image, animalistic references and mythology aside, he is, after all, just twenty years old. Though physically more imposing than official programs advertise (6'4", 228 pounds), his straw-colored hair and shy country grin make him look nowhere near as hard as his reputation. In faded blue jeans, hunting shirt and heavy-duty boots appropriate to cow pastures, he appears the genuine farm boy thought to have vanished along with the horse-drawn plow. It seems like the most natural thing in the world when he says, "Football is my whole life."

Soon we are in his room, and Champ Henson is sitting in

176

a small desk chair, his legs half stretched out and shirtsleeves rolled up, revealing a set of anvil-like forearms. Above him are some record albums, a few books, an Ohio State pennant and lots of football memorabilia. He looks out of place sitting in the chair. He is simply too big for it.

Champ Henson was raised to be a fullback the way some people are raised to be doctors. It was, as far as Champ is concerned, the proper upbringing. Apart from football, there is nothing he would rather talk about than his patriarchal father—a former Ohio Golden Gloves middleweight champion who has kept his Popeye muscles—and those formative years on the farm in Ashville, Ohio.

"It was financially rough," Champ recalls, stretching a leg half-way across the room. "I was the oldest of four boys. We always had plenty to eat but the bathroom was outside and there wasn't any hot water. It was a great place to grow up, though. My dad was the head of the household, the absolute king. It's like with Coach Hayes: When he lays down the law, nobody questions it and that's the way it should be. Too many kids nowadays get to do whatever the hell they want. When we stepped out of line, my dad would let us know it —right up-side the head.

"My dad's biggest dream is to have his sons close to him the rest of his life," Champ goes on. "He's got it all planned out. He's gonna build a big house and each of us—after we make our fortune—we're gonna move in with our wives and children. We'll each get a corner."

At Teays Valley High School, Champ Henson starred at tailback on offense, then switched to defensive end when the ball changed hands. But the school was small and unpublicized and when his senior year arrived, only Michigan, of all places, showed much interest. Champ resigned himself to

Ann Arbor until a friend of his father telephoned Coach Hayes. Within a few days Henson had signed a letter of intent to enroll at Ohio State. Later, when he called Michigan to disclose the decision, assistant backfield coach Chuck Stobart, who had recruited him, blew up and called him a "fuckhead." Champ Henson has had little use for Michigan since.

Champ had a great year in 1972, his sophomore season. By the time the Buckeyes reached Pasadena to prep for their Rose Bowl fiasco against USC, the "animal" image was pretty much out of hand. One West Coast columnist went so far as to suggest that Champ had spent his rustic boyhood days running through chicken-wire fences and murdering baby cattle.

"Americans have become so soft it's pitiful," says Champ, rolling his sleeves up another notch. "If we ever got into another war we'd get our ass kicked. People aren't tough the way they used to be. Students spend most of their time complaining. Even some of the football players do nothing but bitch. Frankly I don't see what the hell any of them have to complain about.

"One thing for sure is people today don't give a shit about other people's problems. I got a lot of friends on the police force and they can tell you stories all day about the way people are these days. Like if a woman is getting raped on the street, people just pass on by without doing anything. They're afraid to get involved. The trouble is that too many people think they can get by just doing this." Snarling, Champ Henson holds up a two-fingered peace signal.

Champ Henson is a rare breed, an anachronism, a young man on a college campus who knows who he is and what he is about. Life is not as complicated for him as it is for many

178

his age. His long-range plans call for him to give pro football a shot—intuition tells him he will be drafted by the New York Jets—and get his master's degree in education. This will qualify him to coach. "I figure I know more about football than anything else," he says, not smiling.

Before the 1973 season it was sometimes said or written that Champ Henson was the best fullback in college football and Champ agrees. "My dad always said, 'Brag like hell and then live up to it,' " he says, still exhibiting a bland countenance. "But I honestly don't think anyone in America can beat me. Some may be quicker and a few may even be stronger. But I can control the middle better and nobody can touch me for running at the goal line. Right now I may not be getting all that much recognition because my average has only been a little over four yards a carry and people who don't know much about football go by averages. But my greatest games are ahead of me. I just know my time is coming."

The injury happens to Champ Henson with thirty-eight seconds left in the first quarter against TCU, the second game of the 1973 season. Henson, taking a handoff, plows into the left side of the line from the TCU 8. He is hit by the middle guard. It is not a sharp hit. The middle guard has him in his arms and Champ Henson is trying to spin away, to lose him. It is a move he makes a dozen times a game. He plants his left leg and begins to pivot as the defensive right end comes slashing across. Champ Henson goes down, disappearing under a pileup of defenders. He is on his back, staring at his left knee as if it has somehow betrayed him. By the time two trainers help him back to the bench, his leg is beginning to stiffen. Soon it is numb, in shock. He feels nothing except a slight burning. "This is it," he gasps. "This is bad." He is pale, sweating. Dr. Joseph Leach, a team physician, rocks the lower leg and hears the knee pop in and out. Champ Henson—"The Animal"—closes his eyes and squeals like a tiny pup.

Later, in the dressing room, Dr. Leach says, "I gotta fix it, Champ."

"Bullshit, you ain't cutting on me, doc," Champ Henson says. "Let me out for two weeks and I'll be all right."

"No, I gotta fix it," the doctor says.

"Do what he says, son," Champ Henson's father says.

Champ Henson, in a whirl of codeine, ice and tape, does not return. But he is not to be missed this day. The Machine rolls, 37–3, with reserves playing most of the second half. Tomorrow the UPI and AP polls of coaches and writers will rank the Ohio State Buckeyes the Number 1 college football team in the nation. Meanwhile in a Columbus hospital, Champ Henson is wheeled into surgery, his knee opened and three stitches knitted into his shredded ligament. Champ Henson is lost for the season to the game he says is his whole life. When he awakens, his father leans over and whispers words that will stay with him through the long autumn days: "This will heal, son, and other people will pay."

The Machine, despite Champ Henson's absence, never slows as it turns toward the rest of its schedule. Dissatisfied with his substitute fullbacks, Woody Hayes dips into his defense and comes up with reserve linebacker Bruce Elia. A one-time All-State fullback from Cliffside Park, New Jersey, Elia, a junior, has not played a minute at the position on the varsity level since arriving in Buckeye country. The transition, however, is orderly. In his first game Elia runs for 2 touchdowns and throws a slew of significant blocks, leading

180

the team to victory over Washington State, 27–3. It isn't a landslide but the Machine delivers as expected. The next Saturday the Buckeyes travel to play Wisconsin, a nuisance team that has made Nebraska and Colorado sweat in previous outings this season. On arrival in Madison, there is a good belly laugh over a local newspaper report that this is to be Woody's last game. President Nixon, it has been learned, is set to nominate him that evening as the next Vice President. The idea, alas, never materializes: Nixon appoints somebody else and Woody Hayes goes back to running his own empire. In the game Archie Griffin outgains the entire Wisconsin backfield in rushing yardage, 169 to 104, and the Buckeyes ramble, 24–0. *Nolo contendere.*

As the season wears on, the Machine continues to operate as efficiently as ever, demolishing opponents Saturday after Saturday. It rolls over Indiana, 37–7, unfazed by the Hoosiers' gimmick-specializing coach, Lee Corso, who brings his team to the stadium in a British double-decker bus. It rolls over Northwestern, 60–0, a thrashing so humiliating that Woody offers some postgame solace to his former pupil, Wildcat coach John Pont. Victory comes again but in numbers less overwhelming the next week against Illinois, whose stubborn defense has helped it run up a 4–0 conference record. It is a "must" game for the Buckeyes, also 4–0 at the time, and they come through, sweeping to a 30–0 win after leading by a nervous 3–0 at halftime. For an injury-wracked and lackluster Michigan State team the next Saturday, Hayes prepares surprisingly hard. He is angry at having misjudged the strength of the Spartans two years in a row, resulting in losses, and he wants to reassert the Machine's superiority. Michigan State, unable to get its second first down until the middle of the fourth quarter, is crushed, 35–0. Against a pathetic Iowa team the next week, the 55–13 landslide is a relatively modest reflection of Ohio State's true domination.

Through its first nine games, the Machine wins bigger than ever before. The Buckeye offense proves to be an unstoppable phalanx, rushing for a school record of 3,354 yards, scoring 46 touchdowns and averaging 40.1 points a game. Meanwhile the defense ranks as college football's stingiest, posting 4 shutouts, allowing 2.7 points a game and even outscoring its nine foes combined, 5 touchdowns to 4. At no time in any game has Ohio State been behind. The Number 1 rating has been kept intact.

All of this, however, is not important now. Next week, the tenth game of the season, the Buckeyes will be playing their hated rivals, the team from the University of Michigan. Almost without exception in the last half-dozen years, Ohio State has played this essentially one-game season. This year the Machine's test will be no different. Once again the results and statistics of the nine other games can be discarded. Once again the season will come down to this sixty-minute blood-letting with Michigan, also unbeaten and untied. This is not just the most important game of the season. This *is* the season, time to turn up the hole cards and show the aces, and the pot has never been sweeter in the rivalry's seventy-game history. Winning will mean the national championship, the Big Ten title, another trip to the Rose Bowl and the prestige and recruiting leverage that go with such spoils. Losing will mean disaster. A political machine cannot survive if it captures the primaries and goes down in the general elections.

The game would have been big if it had just matched complete strangers under these conditions, instead of bringing together two such dedicated enemies. Ohio State and Michigan had enjoyed a steadily growing, good old-fashioned college hatred since 1897, the year they first met on the gridiron. But the seeds of the rivalry are said to have been planted all the way back in 1835, when the states of Ohio and Michigan declared war on each other. Then, as now, the dispute was over territory, each side claiming the land in and around the city of Toledo. The fighting ended when President Andrew Jackson arranged a compromise giving Toledo to Ohio but appeasing Michigan by offering the now valuable Northern Peninsula, taking it away from Wisconsin, which didn't seem to care.

Probably the most famous OSU–Michigan football game took place in 1950. The contest is remembered less for its outcome than for the circumstances under which it was played—a driving snowstorm that closed down the Midwest. The Blizzard Bowl, as it has come to be known, was won by Michigan, 9–3, when a punt by Ohio State's Vic Janowicz was blocked and a Michigan player fell on the ball in the Buckeyes' end zone. It was the only time in memory a team had won a football game without once making a first down. Though both sides were, as usual, strong defensively, the weather had a lot to do with the absence of offense. It was so cold that day that band members' lips peeled when they touched the mouthpieces of their instruments, and all players, even the quarterbacks, wore gloves. The snow was so dense and the wind that carried it so strong that play could not be followed from the stands. None of this stopped fifty thousand people from showing up at Ohio Stadium that day and staying to the final whistle.

That's the way the rivalry was when Woody Hayes became coach in 1951, and it was even more intense now in 1973. Under Hayes the Buckeyes had whipped the Wolverines eleven out of fifteen times between 1954 and 1968, reversing a long period of Michigan supremacy. It was only after Michigan hired Glen E. "Bo" Schembechler, a former Hayes player and assistant coach, that the balance began to tip back. Schembechler promptly won two of four from his old teacher, aided by a large number of talented athletes he had personally recruited in Ohio.

Aside from such ironies, the rivalry had been fueled in recent years by the contrasting images and attitudes of the two schools and the towns where they are located. On the surface both are sprawling state institutions with acres of shiny steel and concrete buildings and overflowing parking lots. But the differences are considerable. Michigan, drawing more than one-third of its thirty-two thousand students from outside the state, is cosmopolitan in the backgrounds, nationalities, colors and politics of its enrolled pupils. Ohio State, a bigger school but with a much smaller percentage of out-of-state students, is far more conformist, conservative, vocational and culturally limited. Ann Arbor, a progressive college town of a hundred thousand with an unusual municipal tolerance for eccentricity had, until the state overrode it, one of the most liberal drug laws in the country, limiting the penalty for marijuana possession to a five-dollar fine. Such leniency would be out of the question in Columbus, where the police department still maintains one of the largest anti-drug units outside the Federal Drug Enforcement Administration.

The game, then, had evolved into a kind of social conflict. It was Michigan, forward-looking and academically prestigious, versus Ohio State, hidebound and scholastically unglamorous; Scotch versus beer drinkers; salon society versus the lunch-bucket crowd. To steadfast Ohio State, Michigan represented nothing more than a collection of phony intellec-

184

tuals with overblown academic reputations and Ivy League pretensions. To ambitious Michigan, Ohio State will never denote anything more than it was at its beginning, a preparatory school for farmers.

The opposing styles of the two schools did not extend to their football coaches. Schembechler had played tackle for Hayes at Miami of Ohio in 1949 and 1950, then had served as his offensive line coach at Ohio State from 1958 to 1963. He was a forty-three-year-old, slightly slimmed-down version of his mentor with none of the charisma, bookishness or broad interests, but much of the abrasiveness, dogmatism, inner fury, stress on fundamental football, unquenchable passion for work and explosive temper. One time when Hayes threw a chair at him during a coaches' meeting, Schembechler just picked it up and threw it back. As an individual, Bo Schembechler did not appear to be any more different from Woody Hayes than Alaric the Goth was from Attila the Hun. He was so faithful a copy of the original that Big Ten people had taken to calling him—to his chagrin— "Little Woody" and "a chip off the old Woody." But by any standard, Schembechler deserved to be rated among the most successful coaches in America. He had produced winners, molded All-Americans and gotten consistently brutal effort from his players. In five years at Michigan, he had revitalized the long-dormant alumni recruiting organization, doubled the football budget and won forty-eight out of fifty-four games. He had learned well at his master's knee. Schembechler had built his own machine.

The small banquet room was getting crowded. But like any room Woody Hayes enters, there was no question that it was his room. He sat down in the seat that had been saved for him at the head table, picked up a spoon and began eating his fruit cup. Next to his plate there was a cake that said BEAT MICHIGAN in gray icing and a scarlet-and-gray striped tie in a box. But he was too preoccupied to pay any attention to the gifts. The eyes of the crowd were turning toward him and the sportswriters were grabbing their notebooks in anticipation of his first words. But Hayes did not seem to notice and kept right on eating.

"Watch out for Woody this week," a sportswriter whispered. "He'll be so tight he'll squeak."

That is the way it always is the week Ohio State plays Michigan, the game they call, in Columbus, THE GAME. Columbus calendars revolve around the Michigan game the way Western calendars center on the birth of Jesus Christ. People speak of a baby being born, say, five days before the Michigan game of 1967, or of a restaurant opening three days after the Michigan game of 1971—"B.M." and "A.M." To Woody Hayes, it's an event that means far more than any other.

This was the Monday before the game, the regular weekly press luncheon in a basement banquet room of the Jai Lai restaurant, and three dozen sportswriters and broadcasters from around the country were waiting for Woody to say something. It was different from previous Monday luncheons. The air was tight with nervous chewing and muted talk. "I'm getting jittery myself," one of the writers said. "This is like the Last Supper."

Hayes, wearing a biscuit-brown jacket, beige tie and silver-rimmed glasses, looked as if he wanted to be anywhere but here. He finished the fruit cup and began eating his salad, still oblivious to the eyes in the room. A local radio reporter sitting about ten feet away leaned over and switched on a tape recorder. Frowning, Hayes looked up from his salad and pointed toward the man. "Let's not turn that on till I get ready to talk. Okay?" The radio reporter bowed his head and turned the recorder off. "Is it off now?" Hayes demanded. The reporter stammered assurances that it was.

An Ohio State publicity man bent over and whispered into Hayes's left ear, cupping his mouth with his hand so the newsmen, who were all straining to catch the words, would not be able to hear. Woody nodded. The publicity man, who was in his twenties and had short hair and a jowly face, stood up.

"Practice will be closed this week," the publicity man said in the loud, flat, self-important tones of a low-ranking army officer. "However, Coach Hayes has agreed to meet with the press fifteen minutes after the conclusion of practice at the North Facility."

Finally Woody Hayes himself rose to his feet and cleared his throat. "Now gentlemen, a good general doesn't announce his weaknesses. So we're not going to talk about our injuries today," he said. "Sorry we have to close practice, but if we let one guy in we have to let everybody and one guy can let out what we're doing."

The sportswriters had been telling funny stories about Woody and his closed practices before he arrived. During Michigan week the year before, one writer recalled, Hayes was putting his team through a secret scrimmage at the North Facility practice field, when he noticed something awry. The field, surrounded by a tall, tarpaulin-covered fence, sits across a four-lane highway from a university-owned hotel and convention meeting place called the Fawcett Center for Tomorrow. The field is roughly five hundred yards from the hotel, yet somehow Hayes had managed to

187

spot something he didn't like in a room on the tenth floor. He called the campus police. The cops rushed up to the room and found a devoted Michigan fan busily filming the practice with a telephoto lens.

Paul Hornung, the Columbus *Dispatch* sports editor, said he personally preferred closed practices. Hornung said he was afraid if he were allowed in, he "might write something that would be detrimental to the team." The other reporters did not seem to mind being shut out either. There was not a murmur of protest over the announcement. Michigan was doing the same thing, it was noted.

"Are there any questions I can pass over today?" Hayes was saying now.

"Coach, can we get up too high for a game like this?" a Columbus newsman asked.

"Sure we can get up too high," Woody replied. "We can get up too early. We can get up too late, too. But we'll be ready."

Then Hayes impatiently answered a few more questions from the writers and broadcasters who sometimes said "we" instead of "you" when referring to Ohio State.

Less than five minutes after he had first stood up, Woody Hayes was gone. He had cut off a reporter in midquestion, held up his hand and with a brusque "Okay, men," stalked out. He did not even stay to get his piece of the cake that said BEAT MICHIGAN.

By Monday evening after practice he had loosened up a little, leading a train of writers into a small office inside the team training room. He was wearing a red windbreaker, cleats and a whistle on a string around his neck. He still hadn't smiled, but he was the perfect host, ordering orange juice all around and seeing to it that everybody had a chair.

Then he sat behind a desk and talked. "Our kids did pretty well today," he began. "We had a good practice."

A Chicago writer asked a question about Cornelius Greene, the quarterback, and Hayes said he would be held out of practice until Wednesday to rest his knee. The disclosure came as a surprise. Nothing had been said earlier of the injury. Had the good general announced a weakness? Or was it a coach's red herring, designed to confuse an opponent?

A student reporter asked Hayes how strong the Wolverines were on defense and Woody snapped: "I'm not going to even talk about Michigan. They're a fine football team. They've proved it."

Until now he had not even mentioned the word *Michigan* and he would not again the rest of the week. The very word is distasteful to him. Over the years he has cultivated a half-funny, half-serious loathing for "the school up north" and its state. It is said that he once coasted across the Michigan–Ohio state line with an empty gas tank rather than patronize a Michigan gas station and contribute to the state's tax coffers. In Hayes's view Ohio boys who enroll at Michigan, especially football players, are either traitors or degenerates, or both. Sometimes it's hard to tell if he's kidding when he talks about Michigan. The consensus is that he isn't.

Woody looked a little tired now but he stayed behind the desk and kept answering questions. The inevitable funny question arose, the one about passing. It was a stock question the writers never tired of asking because they knew it would get a humorous response that would make good copy and wouldn't get him angry. Even in this they belonged to him. They were his straight men.

"Coach, Michigan was eighth in the Big Ten against the pass this year," a reporter started, unable to suppress a grin.

"Does that mean you'll be passing a lot?"

"Hell, yes," boomed football's most celebrated conservative, right on cue. "We're gonna pass 'em right off the field." As always, the writers roared and scribbled his answer in their notebooks.

Then Hayes spoke of his favorite players. The names that came up were the same ones that had been coming up all year —John Hicks, Archie Griffin, Brian Baschnagel. Hicks, of course, was a coach's dream: not just a great All-American player, but also a cheerleading company man on and off the field. Griffin and Baschnagel, though markedly different in ability, were similar as individuals. They were almost too good to be true—unfailingly polite, kind, well groomed, soft spoken, considerate, unflinchingly loyal, somewhat shy, completely dedicated and reverent toward authority. It was not difficult to understand Coach Hayes's affection for these two sophomores. Baschnagel, the wingback, had missed the three previous games because of knee trouble and Hayes reported that he was back and running well.

"I'm surprised at that Brian Baschnagel—the way he's healed up," Woody said. "It's amazing. He and Arch are like old men—they work so hard. I've never seen kids take coaching like that."

"Are old men known for working hard?" I asked.

"Yah, y' see, there isn't much else to do," he replied, allowing himself a smile for the first time all day. "I'll probably get hell from our senior citizens now."

"You seem to be in a pretty good mood," I said.

"Naw, I'm not in such a good mood," he answered with a mock grimace. "If you don't watch it, I might just jump down your throat."

On Tuesday he was still in high spirits. The team had been

190

practicing at the stadium, and to accustom the offensive players to the huge adversary throng they would face in Ann Arbor, Woody had arranged for recorded crowd noise to be piped in. The din could be heard in many parts of campus.

From one end of town to the other, people were getting up for the game. Conversations began and ended with the subject of football. Stores, large and small, plastered their windows with signs urging Ohio State on. Almost every car carried a pro-Buckeye bumper sticker, ranging in inspiration from BUCK BO TWO IN A ROW to DUMP GARBAGE IN ANN ARBOR. Disc jockeys flooded the airwaves with pap about the game and told insult jokes about Michigan. There were rallies, marches and parties—all swirling around this one football game.

Woody Hayes did not have time for any of the trifles. He did not even have time to go home. Every waking minute— and there weren't many sleeping ones—was now dedicated to the game: watching and rewatching films, digesting the statistics, adjusting the game plan, structuring workouts, smoothing out the arrangements for the trip to Ann Arbor, preparing, planning, plotting. Not overlooking one detail. It was one thing for the people of Columbus to demand that Ohio State win. It was another to be the man who had to deliver the victory.

Back at the North Facility on Tuesday Woody was once again suffering the presence of the press. He talked about the fullback he had lost, Champ Henson, and the one he had found, Bruce Elia. "Bruce has done a real fine job for us, but Champ"—his voice trailed off—"Champ would have been a great runner for us this season. Nobody runs at the goal line like Champ."

I mentioned that Iowa coach Frank Lauterbur, the man

191

Hayes had routed three days earlier, had been fired that afternoon. Iowa hadn't won a game all year but athletic officials there were insisting that the dismissal had come because of Lauterbur's refusal to "realign" his coaching staff. Had Woody heard about it? What was his reaction? He looked back at me sharply.

"No, I didn't know," he said, straightening up in his chair. "But I *despise* people who fire coaches while the season is still on. They have no goddamned right to do it. I'll bet he could take it to court and win."

Hayes stood up, his face flushed. "Now I'm mad," he shouted. "I'm bitter about that. Frank Lauterbur's a helluva man, a helluva coach and he's got a good Marine record, too."

The words were coming out in a torrent now. "And you can bet the reason given is a *damn lie.* The reason he got fired is he didn't win enough ball games. Let's face it. Why can't they be honest about it and say he didn't win so we fired him? They've got to come up with some phony picayune reason. I *despise* people like that. Not in the middle of the goddamned season."

On Wednesday Woody was tired. One glance at him, red-eyed, slumping in his chair, and it was apparent that the pressures of the week, the intensity of the work, were beginning to show. "We wound up our hard practice tonight," he said, not bothering to stifle a yawn. His voice was flat with fatigue. "Listen, fellas. I don't want to miss dinner with the team again. I've missed it the last couple of nights wasting my time here with you." He looked dolefully around the room at the sportswriters. "So that's it." That was it.

Thursday was Thanksgiving, sunny and warm and a beautiful day for the "senior tackle." This is a fifty-year-old ritual in which all the seniors on the team hurl themselves at a tackling dummy in Ohio Stadium, a stylized farewell before their final game. Such customs at most schools have long since gone into the earth.

By 1:30 P.M., a half-hour before the senior tackle was scheduled to start, a crowd of several thousand people had gathered at the stadium gates and was being held back by policemen. They could have stayed home to watch Thanksgiving Day football on television. Instead they were at Ohio Stadium to witness a Buckeye sacrament.

Before long the crowd was sitting in the stadium's wooden bleachers and cheering as wildly as if a real game were at hand. The seniors were lined up along the sideline, awaiting this final passage into manhood. Woody's voice thundered into the air through a bullhorn.

"Awright now I've told the fellas not to hit too hard today," he roared. "Back in 1956 a fella by the name of Jim Roseboro, who is now Councilman Roseboro, hit it so hard that he ruptured a rib and ended up fumbling three times in the big game."

The fans let out a groan at the awful memory. Woody, though, was chuckling. It had happened seventeen years ago and he could afford to laugh about it now. "So we're not gonna hit it too hard today but we'll hit it hard enough to make it pop a little bit," he promised.

One by one, as in a graduation ceremony, the seniors marched up and shook hands with Coach Hayes, who called out their names through his bullhorn and gave the signal for them to run up and smash into the gray tackling dummy ten yards away. As they waited their turn most of the seniors did not seem to be taking the ritual seriously. Some giggled and snickered; a few looked embarrassed and shifted self-consciously. But Woody was addressing the crowd and did not seem to notice.

The offense went first, and Hayes was not enthusiastic about the execution. "These are all offensive men so they don't know how to tackle too well," he said. Then it was the defense's turn. Randy Gradishar, the All-American linebacker, came up for his shot, and the fans gave him a standing ovation. Gradishar, looking ill at ease, hit the dummy without much force. "He's the best linebacker we've had in twenty-three years," bellowed Hayes, "and from the looks of that tackle he's saving it all for Saturday."

Finally only one senior was left. "Senior linebacker Rick Middleton," Woody shouted into the bullhorn, as the crowd cheered. "I recruited this fella in a pizza joint in Delaware, Ohio."

Unlike his teammates, Middleton held nothing back. He ran hard, lowered his shoulder and flung himself like a rock at the dummy, sending it into a fifteen-yard skid. It was by far the day's most ferocious collision, and Hayes, forgetting that it didn't count, exclaimed, "Nice hit, Rick."

Later, back at the training facility, the seniors and the other team members were coming out of the locker room. Many of them were in blue jeans and boots and their hair was long and shaggy. Outside, two buses were waiting to take them to a nearby Holiday Inn for Thanksgiving dinner and an evening of meetings and football on television. Several players stopped to look at a bulletin board, which Hayes had covered with articles about the Michigan game of 1969. That was the year one of his great Buckeye teams had gone through the season unbeaten. They were ranked Number 1 in the polls and were riding a twenty-two-game winning streak into the last game. Then, in Ann Arbor, the team lost

24–12. Four years later and still that day of infamy had to be avenged—by players who'd been in high school at the time.

Woody Hayes, naked, came out of the shower and strode past the bulletin board down the corridor into his office. Walking almost alongside, also nude and fresh from the shower, was defensive tackle Pete Cusick, a weight-lifting devotee of Charles Atlas and probably the strongest man on the team. Kaye Kessler of the *Citizen-Journal* watched the odd couple come and go and deadpanned, "There go two great physiques."

"We've probably prepared more minutely for this game than any we've ever played," said Hayes, dressed now and sitting behind his desk in the coaches' meeting room. "We know their personnel, their formations and their plays almost as well as our own."

Someone mentioned that the biggest crowd in college football history was expected on Saturday and Hayes grinned. "Well, you know [Michigan athletic director] Don Canham says, 'Woody Hayes is worth thirty thousand tickets a game so I guess I can pay for the down markers he breaks.' You know what my answer is to him? He can pay for the down markers but *I'll* hire the referees."

As Hayes talked, John Hicks came into the meeting room. Hicks had come down with a slight case of the flu and Hayes was worried about his star lineman.

"John, how do you feel today?" Woody asked.

"Feel pretty good," Hicks replied.

"Well, damnit, say so!"

"I feel pretty good, sir."

"Well then *act* that way too. You haven't been up to snuff all this week, John. I'm disappointed in you."

195

"I haven't been feeling good, sir. Had flu."

"I know. I know. But you're about over it now, aren't you?"

"Yes, sir."

"This is going to be your greatest game."

"By far."

"Why don't you get up and tell us that Saturday?"

"I'll tell you that anytime."

"Tell it to the team then will you, John? Then challenge Kregel! Challenge Pagac! Let's get 'em on fire!"

Friday. A day for travel. Sunny, temperatures in the sixties, almost no wind. Right away it was clear that in Ann Arbor the game was far less a life-and-death matter. There was a sign in a restaurant window that said SAVE FUEL, BURN WOODY and another one that said IMPEACH WOODY, but for the most part, banners, bumper stickers and other visual hoopla were hard to find on campus. "The students up here root for the team and go to the games," Dan Boris, the sports editor of the *Michigan Daily,* said later. "But they aren't fanatics like the Ohio students. There's more than football going on up here."

The mounting pressure of the game had transformed the Buckeyes into an unusually grim-looking group on their arrival in Ann Arbor. The team was further troubled by the news, which everyone tried to keep secret, that Cornelius Greene was still not in the best of shape. The problem was not his knee, as had been reported, but the thumb on his passing hand, which had been jammed in the Iowa game and had not responded to treatment. Normally swaggering and loose, the team marched into the downtown Ramada Hotel with rigid expressions that did not suggest confidence. Jim

Kregel, the resourceful offensive guard and bantering Alex Karras–type extrovert, was uncommunicative and solemn as he went up to his room for the afternoon nap. Later the players would go for a walk, attend meetings, eat a steak dinner, see a movie, and be brought milk and cookies in their rooms before going to bed at ten o'clock for the last time before the Michigan game.

Selecting a suitable film was, as always, a ticklish matter. Hayes automatically ruled out anything that might sexually stir his players, and that didn't leave many contemporary movies to choose from. His designated "movie scout," backfield coach Rudy Hubbard, had narrowed the choice down to *Billy Jack,* a modern Western the team had already seen twice before, and *Executive Action,* an account of President Kennedy's assassination that theorized conspiracy.

"If you go see that, I just want you to know it's a damn lie," Woody told the players at dinner. "What the Warren Commission said was right. Lee Harvey Oswald was no radical. He was a hater who acted alone." The team went to see *Billy Jack.*

Later that night, long after Hayes and his players had gone to bed, several Ohio State assistant coaches and athletic department staffers were sitting in the hotel's rooftop bar, drinking, trying to relax. "We've never stayed at this place before," someone said. "Every time we lose Woody switches hotels."

Everybody laughed and a reporter brought up the Hayes tradition of serving the players milk and cookies in bed. "Hey, man, don't knock it," said Dick Delaney, an assistant athletic director. "It works. Woody wins."

Defensive coordinator George Hill had been sitting quietly for some time, lost in thought and drinking beer. But now as he got up to leave he rubbed his hands feverishly and said: "This is gonna be some sonofabitch. This is what it's all about. This is what you live for."

Saturday brought a slow chill drip of rain. Overcast skies painted midmorning in the dark colors of twilight. Funeral weather.

Ohio State's Buckeyes were standing now in the Ramada lobby after being gathered from the rooms where they had been locked up since ten o'clock the night before. Perhaps because it was expected of them, but then perhaps not, they wore grotesquely somber expressions. The air was full of quick breaths and snapping chewing gum. Anne Hayes, usually chatty and outgoing, looked pale and tense. She was sitting by herself and her salt-and-pepper hair was pulled back in a bun with a red ribbon. "You know, even after all these years," she said softly, "you still worry before every game." At 10:45 Woody Hayes came out of an elevator, marched toward the front door and announced, "This rain won't hurt us a damn bit." Then the Buckeyes were in their buses, led by state-police cars and careening toward Michigan Stadium.

The rain had stopped by the time the two teams ran onto the field for warmups an hour before the game. At one end of the mammoth oval stadium the Ohio State rooters, about ten thousand strong, were already in their seats whooping it up. Champ Henson, out of uniform and limping slightly, came down the runway from the locker room. He was snorting air like a heavyweight fighter, maniacally clenching and unclenching his fist, and his face was as red as his OSU jacket. Then Woody Hayes, chewing gum like a rabbit, trotted out on the field, and suddenly the giant Michigan crowd,

198

quiet until now, erupted into a bedlam of boos.

Soon there would be 105,223 people in the stadium, the most ever to come to a regular season college football game. The Ohio State marching band came out on the field and in the stands the Buckeye faithful screamed their hearts out and sang: *Oh, we don't give a damn for the whole state of Michigan. We're from Ohio.* The Michigan band came out next, playing its fight song, "Hail to the Victors," and the far larger but not much louder Michigan crowd went into chants of "Go Blue." Then the players were back on the field jumping all over each other and the noise was enough to knot the stomach. Through it all Coach Hayes stood on the sidelines, hands on hips, waiting for the game to start.

For months now it had been steadily blown up into the biggest college match of the year. Aside from other Ohio State–Michigan clashes, the last game in the Midwest to create such a prekickoff frenzy had been Notre Dame versus Michigan State in 1966. That contest, billed as the Game of the Decade, had also brought together undefeated, untied teams with tickets going for one hundred dollars and hordes of sportswriters descending from all over. That game too had been dominated by freak plays, injuries and odd coaching judgments. That game had ended in a tie, 10–10.

It was impossible to tell beforehand how this Ohio State–Michigan game would go. The Wolverines, ranked Number 4, appeared only a little less talented and physically imposing than the Buckeyes. Except for a relatively narrow escape against Illinois, they had brushed aside ten straight opponents almost as easily as Ohio State had, renewing charges from critics of the Big Ten that the conference should really be called "the Big Two and the Little Eight." The Michigan defense, led by All-American tackle Dave Gallagher and

199

safetyman Dave Brown, had allowed only 5.8 points a game, swarming over foes in the same way as Ohio State, stunting, squirming, sliding, penetrating, hitting and forcing mistakes. On offense, too, Michigan behaved amazingly like Ohio State, operating out of an I formation, emphasizing a punishing ground game with a hard-running fullback, Ed Shuttlesworth, and guided by a quick and sharp ball-handling black quarterback, Dennis Franklin.

Even if the Buckeyes had the edge in personnel, and the experts agreed they did, it was important to remember that Michigan was the home team and the home team had won each of the last six OSU–Michigan games. Under Schembechler Michigan had proved astonishingly tough on its own field, never losing a conference game there.

Then, too, since Schembechler's arrival, the series had taken a bizarre turn. The clear favorite, the best team on paper, had almost always managed to lose. As a 14-point underdog, Schembechler's first Michigan team in 1969 had shocked Number 1–ranked and unbeaten Ohio State in the famous 24–12 upset. Then in 1972 Michigan, favored by four points took a 10–0 record to Columbus, only to be outslugged 14–11. For this, the rubber match between the old coach and his protégé, the Buckeyes had emerged the 3½-point choice of the bookies.

The scale of pros and cons, strengths and weaknesses, advantages and disadvantages, seemed in near-perfect balance. Ohio State had the better punter and punt-return game; Michigan, the better place kicker. Ohio State had the better offensive line; Michigan, the better defensive line. Ohio State had the better running; Michigan, the better passing. Neither team could pass much, the smart money figured, but both might be able to pass if the defenses stacked the line too much. Each team was finally getting around to picking on someone its own size. Yet the last thing on anyone's mind was a tie.

For the first quarter it looked like the two teams would never unwind and act like the Number 1 and Number 4 organizations they were supposed to be. Michigan's Shuttlesworth did manage several impressive blasts up the middle for first downs, but for the most part the runners on both sides went nowhere, primarily because of Gradishar and Cusick of the Buckeyes and Brown and linebacker Steve Strinko of the Wolverines. In three possessions, Ohio State was unable to move, did not scratch out one first down. Archie Griffin gained just ten yards on his first seven carries. Even though he was running behind an unusual eight-man line that Hayes thought would traumatize Michigan, Griffin did not come close to breaking clear. When OSU's Tom Skladany punted weakly to the Wolverines' 47, giving them good field position, Michigan countered with a fumble, then a delay penalty and a clip. The passing was just as poor, with two of Franklin's three passes sailing atrociously off-target and Greene, his thumb in a bandage, abstaining altogether. It looked like two ancient dinosaurs flailing at each other.

On the opening play of the second quarter, just as it appeared that the Buckeyes would stall again, Griffin darted through a hole on the right side of the line, cut back to the middle and outran a cluster of maize-and-blue jerseys for 38 yards until safetyman Brown, a wrench in the Buckeye works all day, angled him down from behind at the Michigan 34. Six battering ground plays later, despite merciless double-team blocking on Gallagher out of the Robust alignment, the Buckeyes were stopped and place kicker Blair Conway came in and kicked a 31-yard field goal. It was 3–0 and suddenly the Michigan crowd was very quiet.

Ohio State scored again with fifty-three seconds left in the quarter, this time crossing the goal line with a meticulously brutal ground-bound drive befitting the Machine. From the Ohio State 45, Griffin fired through four straight times for 6, 7, 7 and 12 yards. Pete Johnson, the burly freshman fullback in for Elia, hammered the middle for 9 yards down to the Michigan 14. Griffin smashed over left tackle for 9 yards. Then it was Johnson again, crashing through the left side and carrying Gallagher and two other Michigan tacklers for 5 yards into the end zone, a display of individual packhorse power that the Buckeyes had not shown since the fall of Champ Henson. As the half ended it seemed clear that Woody Hayes was to be a winner again.

But it did not turn out that way for a number of reasons, not the least of which was Woody Hayes himself. It was as if he had said to himself in the halftime locker room, "Damnit we've got to protect this lead and not make any goddamned mistakes." The Buckeyes made no mistakes, save lack of coaching imagination. They drew no penalties, committed no fumbles, and, up to the game's final minute when panic set in, threw no interceptions. Yet for all their errorlessness they did not score the rest of the afternoon. Ed Ferkany, Ohio State's popular offensive-line coach, thought he knew why. "No matter how good you are, you can't beat a good team not varying your attack," he muttered disgustedly in the gloom of the flight back to Columbus. "We played it too damn conservative."

"Conservative" was not the word for it. Even Woody's stodgy game plan of the first half proved too radical for him in the second half. The master planner, the man who had prepared so "minutely" for this game, actually abandoned his game plan in that second half. Johnson, the bruising fullback who had caused Michigan to grieve in the first half, carried just once in the second. The wingback counter play, a Buckeye staple all year, was not called at all. Quarterback Greene, the game-breaking runner, also carried the ball far less than usual, and despite obvious passing situations, did not throw a single pass all day.

"We must never allow the defense to bunch up on us," Hayes wrote in *You Win With People!* "So we must be able to use broad-front tactics like General Billy Sherman marching through the South and force our opponents to defend both the width and depth of the field." Billy Sherman would have been ashamed of General Woody this day.

For the people who watched it under the cold dreary clouds of Michigan Stadium, or in their cozy living rooms on national television, it made no sense at all. For the assistant coaches who proposed plays from their press-box perches high above the field, it made no sense at all. Ralph Staub, the head man in the coaches' booth, kept sending in plays. They were plays the Buckeyes had practiced all week. They were plays that had worked for them all year. "Let's put the ball in the air, Coach," Staub would say, or "How about a counter play with the wingback, Coach?" or "How about the option here, Coach?" And Woody Hayes kept pulling his cap down harder and harder on his head and saying: "Fuck that fucking play!" "Fuck that fucking play!" "Fuck that fucking play!"

It might have made sense to Woody to run Archie Griffin, certainly as classy a runner as 1973 produced, on almost every play of the second half. It might have been the safe percentage gambit, even with Michigan pinching in more and more on each play to stop him. In the terror of the hour, it might have seemed like the only sane and logical thing to do, and Woody would be willing to carry the argument that he was right to his grave. Woody Hayes, who had wanted to win this game so intensely, so desperately, had not allowed his team to give him that victory. There was an element of tragedy in that.

There was much to say for Michigan's defense, spearheaded by Dave Brown, the busy safetyman, and Steve Strinko, the linebacker. They flatly disregarded the possibility of any kind of pass and, because of Ohio State's attack, never had to pay for it. Jamming the line with eight men, the Wolverines managed to pound out a draw with the formidable Buckeye front wall. This seemed equivalent to mixing it up evenly with George Foreman. They never did stop the brilliant Griffin, who ran 30 times for 163 yards, squirming, bouncing, caroming, breaking more tackles in one game than most runners do in a career. But they smothered him, gang-tackled him, jumped up and down on him and tore at his limbs all day and that helped limit his effectiveness when he might have hurt them most. Woody took care of the rest himself, running the fresh legs off his superb tailback.

On nine rushing plays the Wolverines held the Buckeyes to no gain or minus yardage. They held Cornelius Greene, as good as any quarterback in the country on the wide keeper, to 32 yards on 8 carries. They held Greene, in fact, on what everyone agreed later was the afternoon's watershed play, the one that turned the game around. It occurred on a fourth down and 2 at the Michigan 34-yard line late in the third quarter, with the Buckeyes driving for the clinching score. The call was for a Griffin sweep to the wide side, but Greene, standing over center, noticed everybody in a maize-and-blue helmet leaning that way. The quarterback handled the snap, took the step he always took on the Griffin sweep, then suddenly changed his mind, pivoted and cut back to the other side of the line. Though not an audible, as reported later, it was a smart maneuver. The Michigan defense was slanted to the wide side and the hole was there. But at the last possible moment, Jeff Perlinger, Michigan's hulking tackle, lunged and caught Greene below the knee. It was one of the afternoon's gentlest bumps. But the blow put Greene down, a yard short of the first down. "Damn," mumbled Champ Henson, sitting high up in the Ohio State section. "Damn! Damn!"

For the remainder of the game, it looked as if Michigan were the only team in the stadium. The Wolverines were quicker in the line, truer in execution, more confident in their game plan and more inventive in their attack. With passes, pitchouts and the pounding, trampling runs of Shuttlesworth, they drove from their own 33 down to the Ohio State 12. On the second play of the fourth quarter, Mike Lantry, their fine left-footed place kicker, hoisted a 30-yard field goal. The score: 10–3.

It was on their next possession that quarterback Franklin revved up the tying drive. Shuttlesworth continued to hurt Ohio State with short, stabbing runs, and when the Buckeye linebackers pulled in toward the middle to stop them, Franklin hit passes over their outstretched hands. This was the very thing the Buckeyes were *not* doing to the Wolverine linebackers. Now it was fourth and 1 on the Ohio State 10-yard line—the kind of play that made Hayes yank his cap down over his ears. The call was perfect. Franklin faked a handoff to Shuttlesworth off tackle, freezing the linebackers, and scampered around right end into the end zone. No one touched him.

By now the look of the game, the look of the season, had completely changed. The Machine, unquestionably the superior force in the first half, unquestionably the superior force in its first nine games, did not seem so invincible anymore. Michigan had fought back, had found the soft underbelly of the Ohio State defense. It was all even. And now, with nine minutes and thirty-two seconds remaining, unless the Machine changed its tactics, it appeared that the wrong side would surely win.

The Machine did not. For reasons that puzzled and perplexed nearly every player and coach on his team, Coach Hayes stubbornly stayed on the ground and called for the beleaguered Griffin to carry on every play. Even as the Michigan defenders bunched together in anti-Griffin formations and called the plays in their huddle that they knew the Buckeyes were calling in their own, Woody kept running Griffin into the line, where the big game had been contested to a standoff all afternoon. No one really expected Woody Hayes to step out of character in those desperate moments. No one really expected him to go rococo and start throwing the ball all over the field. But everybody expected him to vary his attack, just as Schembechler had varied *his* attack. And when Griffin kept gouging at the line, some Buckeyes thought themselves victims of their coach's ego trip.

"We couldn't believe it," an Ohio State player said afterward. "We only ran three different plays the whole second half. Shit, they weren't even looking for anything but Archie. We could've scored on them easy if we'd thrown the ball or mixed it up a little. But Woody not only has to beat a team —he has to beat them down. He has to brutalize the other team. That's what he thinks football is all about. It wounds his pride to pass. It's like admitting weakness."

206

"Our passing has not been good," Hayes argued later, staring at the dressing-room floor while reporters pressed him for explanations. "I can tell you that now. I couldn't during the season. It has *not* been satisfactory."

Perhaps. But then why had he done nothing to develop it? Why had he allowed Cornelius Greene to throw only thirty-eight times all season? Why had he kept the ball on the ground, game after game, even after the Buckeyes had run up huge leads? As Woody Hayes himself had said after a midseason game: "If you play too close to the vest you're gonna go downhill. You can get yourself in trouble. Your team's gonna slip. If you button up too much, you're getting worse."

But Woody had not heeded his own words. His passing game, which the Buckeyes worked on in practice but never used, amounted to nothing more than a stack of charts with X's and O's. As the season wore on, the charts remained on the shelf, collecting dust, and stayed there through this frightful Michigan game when Coach Hayes buried himself in his own cloud of dust. Even if Greene's thumb had been okay it was hard to imagine that Woody would have played the game much differently. He had made the decision to go after the big game of the year his way, and dared Michigan to stop him. His players and assistant coaches had merely followed orders, at times bitterly.

"Woody choked on us," said an offensive lineman. "He got so tight he wouldn't let us play our game. We blew 'em out that second quarter with Pete Johnson in there. So what does Woody do? He takes Pete out in the third quarter. Why? Because Pete's a freshman and a freshman might make a mistake. What good does it do not to make mistakes if you're not moving the ball?

"Corny's injury just gave Woody another excuse not to pass. If Corny was hurt that bad why didn't he bring in Greg Hare? Greg was the starter when we beat Michigan last year. It's hard to believe a team with our talent couldn't mount some kind of passing attack—a swing pass, a screen pass, *anything.* Even some incompletions. Just enough to keep the other side off balance. We didn't pass all year because we didn't have to and when we had to we didn't because we couldn't. You can't keep a good defense honest with what we did—running one man against the world."

That the one man, Archie Griffin, almost managed to bail his team out was far more a tribute to his enormous skills than to the validity of his coach's strategy. Four straight times the squat tailback stormed into the Michigan line, spinning, twisting, wiggling, feinting, planting his hand to keep from falling, grinding out 29 gnawing yards to the Ohio State 49. But on his last carry, a pickup of 7 yards, Griffin came together with Michigan's Brown in one of the day's most crucial crackups. Brown met Griffin at the ankles, flipping him to the ground, and after the whistle had blown, gave his leg a vicious twist, like a rodeo cowboy about to tie a calf. The maneuver snapped some tendons in Griffin's knee and with Griffin limping off the field, Ohio State's hopes glimmered. The Machine had run aground.

The play enabled Michigan to regain possession and have its chance to win. Franklin marched the Wolverines right back down the field 38 yards to the Buckeye 38. But as he delivered his last pass, defensive end Van DeCree buried his gray helmet in the quarterback's collarbone and broke it. It looked as if Franklin had been smacked by a falling cinder block. The Michigan drive stalled and Schembechler sent in Lantry to try a 58-yard field goal, a distance well within his range. It missed to the left by no more than a yard.

With sixty-one seconds left, Ohio State threw its first pass of the day and it was almost one pass too many. Hayes knew that a tie would cost his team the national championship, to say nothing of the Rose Bowl, and he was going for broke. Greene was taken out and senior cocaptain Greg Hare was told in Woody's doomsday voice to get in there and put that ball in the air. On the first play Hare, backpedaling to escape a rush, floated a weak pass to the left side and Michigan's Tom Drake intercepted it, rambling back 7 yards to the Buckeye 33-yard line. At this point the crowd was delirious, shouting long choruses of "Go-o-o-o Blue-ue-ue-ue," while the band serenaded them with "Hail to the Victors."

The Wolverines ran on first down. Gil Chapman, the tailback, made 6 yards. Then Franklin's substitute, Larry Cipa, hurried his team to the line of scrimmage and threw the ball out of bounds to stop the clock. So it was third down at the Ohio State 27 with twenty-eight seconds left. Out of timeouts and missing his Number 1 quarterback, Schembechler decided not to use his third down. He wanted his kicker to have enough time and he was taking no chances. In came Lantry, a twenty-five-year-old Vietnam veteran who had kicked seven out of ten field goals during the season, including a school record fifty-one-yarder. The kick had to travel forty-four yards. The snap was good and Lantry got the necessary distance into his kick with the aid of a twenty-mile-an-hour wind. But it was wide to the right. Michigan had gotten the big break and blown it.

The game ended and the fans were still in their seats, as if they were waiting for a fifth quarter to be played. Not one person seemed to be leaving the stadium. Not one. Woody Hayes and his team struggled toward their locker room through a knot of Ohio State band members. A young photographer drew alongside, snapping pictures, and Hayes reached over and swatted at him. The blow missed, a gesture of futility as symbolic as the three long desperate passes that ended the game for Ohio State, a team that had thrown only 75 passes all season in its 695 plays.

Later, as the people filed limply through the stadium tunnels, a Michigan coed directed her vacant gaze away from her boyfriend and up toward the scoreboard. It still said 10–10.

"What happens now?" she asked.

"Michigan goes to the Rose Bowl," came his reply, "since Ohio State went last year."

The boyfriend was wrong. Apparently he was not aware that the Big Ten's long-standing ban on a team's making two consecutive Rose Bowl appearances had been lifted in 1971. What had not changed was the league's procedure for breaking a championship tie. Despite calls for a simple solution, such as a sudden-death overtime or statistical formula, conference athletic directors still felt they and they alone were the best judge of who should go to Pasadena. Keeping the verdict in their own hands seemed equivalent to letting the presidents of Detroit's automakers choose the car of the year. No matter who won the vote, there was bound to be lots of indignant grumbling, bickering and charges of politics.

Still, in the aftermath of the big game, everyone figured Michigan would get the athletic directors' nod.

Champ Henson, who had been working out in the hopes of coming back for the Rose Bowl, drove home to Columbus that night, walked into his dorm room and punched a hole clean through the closet door.

Bo Schembechler, claiming Number 1 for his team, said: "We outplayed them and we deserve to go."

Woody Hayes had similar views. "We knew we had to win this one to go and we didn't," he said at his postgame press conference. Later, on his television show, the strain of the turbulent day had begun to show on him. He looked old and his voice cracked a couple of times when he said: "Duffy Daugherty once said a tie is just about as thrilling as kissing your sister. Actually it's not nearly that thrilling. It's just a doggone big disappointment."

John Hicks, standing next to Hayes, talked about his Ohio State football career coming to an end. "Coach, I would like to say something," he said, looking directly into the camera. "It's been great. The organization here is just the greatest in the country. If there are any high school football players looking in right now . . . if you've got a chance to come to Ohio State . . . consider it, really!"

"You're gonna help us recruit, aren't you, John?" said Hayes, his voice suddenly coming back to life.

"Yes, sir," said Hicks.

"You see this is the kind of family we have here," said Hayes. "That's why we hate to see the season end as abruptly as it probably will."

On Sunday morning Big Ten Commissioner Wayne Duke polled the conference athletic directors by telephone and, to nearly everyone's surprise, the vote went to Ohio State. By early afternoon, when the outcome had been made public, the switchboard at the Big Ten office in Chicago exploded with calls, most of them in angry protest. Rarely has any decision in the sports world stirred more bitter controversy, with accusations of low-down politics, scathing newspaper editorials, a class-action suit filed in Federal court and even

211

a speech on the floor of the U.S. House of Representatives. And while many people, particularly in Michigan, were shocked and furious at the vote, the less partisan tended to see it as yet another object lesson showing that the main trouble with college sports is how they are administered.

Schembechler accepted the defeat like the disciple of Woody Hayes he was, lashing out at the athletic directors for voting their "petty jealousies" and at Commissioner Duke for "engineering or at least influencing" the vote. At the age of forty-three the Michigan coach seemed to be making a painful discovery. "The Rose Bowl is supposed to be a reward, an educational experience, and our kids earned it," he told a Michigan *Daily* reporter. "But the directors and Duke were running scared. After losing four straight Rose Bowls they needed a winner to help their prestige. Well the Big Ten has lost any prestige it ever had. I'm disillusioned with the administration of college football. This is why kids are losing respect for America."

For weeks afterward Schembechler continued to scream and holler, hammering away at one theme: decency and fair play versus the corrupt hands of Commissioner Duke and the Big Ten administrators. Since most of them were mediocrities at best, it wasn't a difficult proposition to sell. And Schembechler was encouraged by the support of much of the press—which finally decided that the Big Ten really was a backward-thinking conference—and by the obvious public sympathy outside Ohio. At the peak of his rage Schembechler announced he would accept another bowl bid, although it would violate Big Ten rules, and even threatened to pull out of the conference. But in the end he did nothing, which came as a surprise to no one, and his bombast lost him much of his original backing. In the months after the vote he consoled himself with the big ovations he received at civic luncheons and banquets.

In the face of Schembechler's onslaught, Duke denied any personal maneuvering and asserted that the directors had properly selected—in the words of the conference bylaws— "the most representative team." This euphemism prompted one wag to argue that the choice should have been Northwestern, since the Wildcats finished in a four-way tie for fourth place: ahead of three teams, behind three teams and in a tie with three teams. That was about as representative as a team could get.

Such levity aside, Duke was having a tough time convincing people that politics and personalities had not played a role in the decision. And his insistence on keeping the vote secret did nothing to improve his case or prevent it from coming out later that the result had been 6–4. Many of the athletic directors were known to resent Michigan's successful, high-powered athletic director, Don Canham, a self-made millionaire whose business savvy and talent for selling and promotion were the talk of the college football world. It wasn't that the other directors disliked millionaires. They would let them contribute to their athletic scholarship funds anytime. But in five years Canham had transformed Michigan's floundering sports program into one of the nation's money-making showcases, and he was being widely hailed as the prototype of the new-breed athletic director. Next to Canham, most of the directors looked like candy-store operators and they knew it.

Besides being envious, several directors were said to be nursing grudges against Canham. A man with a habit of stepping on toes and speaking plainly, Canham had more than once publicly referred to his Big Ten counterparts as a "bunch of donkeys." One of them, Northwestern's Tippy Dye, had something more specific to be mad about. Several years earlier, Northwestern had been on the verge of closing a deal to rent its stadium to the Chicago Bears. Canham, thinking that it would set a dangerous business precedent, had led a drive to quash the plan, costing the Big Ten's only private school much-needed revenue. It certainly seemed hard to believe that Dye's vote was not influenced by a desire to get even. Nor did it seem likely that someone like Michigan State's Burt Smith would have voted for Ohio State just because he believed it was the stronger team. Michigan State competes with Michigan for the state's rich output of high school football talent. It is only natural that the Michigan State athletic director would want to deny Michigan the recruiting clout a Rose Bowl appearance brings.

Whatever the real motives of the directors who came through for Ohio State—as well as those who supported Michigan—it was clear that the decision to send the Buckeyes was far less at issue than the way the decision was reached. In the aftermath of the secret poll, questions, doubts and suspicions lingered, mostly because an athletic director is a politician and politicians have axes to grind. Perhaps, as Commissioner Duke and most of the directors insisted, it was true that no politicking had been done by Hayes, Schembechler or any other agent of either school. Perhaps it was true that Duke was not the shrewd, villainous plotter Schembechler portrayed him to be. And perhaps it was true that the directors had been swayed by Franklin's injury, had gone with Ohio State simply because they wanted to win and were nervous after four consecutive Rose Bowl slip-ups. But then why had none of them bothered to contact the Michigan team doctor to ask about Franklin's condition? Why had the decision to select the stronger team been placed in the hands of ten men, eight of whom had not even seen the game? Why the haste with which the vote was taken, with no prior discussion or exchange of views? And why the secrecy, why the refusal to disclose how each man voted, which looked all the more ridiculous when every director eventually did reveal his vote?

One would think that with all the furor raised by the vote, the Big Ten would have wanted to do something about its unfortunate tie-breaking procedure. But with characteristic efficiency, when the directors gathered in Chicago for their regular winter meetings just one week after the game, they failed to come up with a new solution. In fact, Duke unabashedly told reporters, the administrators did not even discuss possible changes. They had traveled their usual course, taking no action at all, except to exonerate Duke of any wrongdoing and authorize him to investigate whether Schembechler should be punished for his intemperate outbursts. Schembechler would have to live with the frowns of his Big Ten brothers.

At first Hayes took the high road in the controversy. While "Little Woody" was hysterical and quarrelsome, "Big Woody" was calm and placating, politely declining to join in the debate. The day the decision came out, he pronounced himself "mighty pleased" and quietly contended that the vote reflected Ohio State's superior performance against common foes, not politics or personalities. He was the model of diplomacy, graciously refusing to comment on Schembechler's ravings about the evil directors, while presenting himself as an island of reason and tranquility. But it was an uncomfortable pose and he shed it three days later when he spoke at a Cincinnati alumni gathering, blasting his former pupil's attitude as "typical of today where every decision is questioned.

"The problem today is we don't accept decisions," he shouted. "I've always accepted decisions." Had the remark been heard by any referees, they might have scratched their heads in disbelief. And while Woody clucked over Schembechler's peevishness, a lot of people who knew him were certain that the same tough words or worse would be coming out of his mouth had circumstances been reversed. Some wondered if his approach would have been limited to harsh words only.

Hayes received word of the vote early Sunday afternoon as he sat in the North Facility meeting room viewing films of the game and waiting for the bad news he was sure would come. Earlier he had made his usual Sunday morning hospital rounds, visiting punter Tom Skladany, whose ankle had been broken in the game on a cheap-shot clip, and several other players nursing assorted limb bruises. His first stop had shaken him badly. As he stepped off the elevator at Riverside Hospital, a nurse told him that Al Hart, his loyal thirty-seven-year-old trainer who had been hospitalized since early in the season with cancer, had died.

Though expected, the news of Hart's death stunned Hayes. As he walked into the North Facility at noon he looked haggard and his eyes showed the strain of the last twenty-four hours. They were glassy and he seemed barely able to keep them open. Aides who saw him that morning say he appeared to be out on his feet, slurring his speech and losing the thread of conversation. While he watched the game films, his head nodded sleepily. Then at 1:30 came the phone call from Ohio State athletic director Big Ed Weaver. It was a squeaker but the one-vote difference was decisive.

216

Michigan's expected sympathy vote had not materialized. The Machine, though slightly tarnished now, was back in the Rose Bowl again.

By late afternoon an exultant, cheering, pushing crowd had gathered outside the house at 1711 Cardiff Road. Police cleared a path for the athletic officials, politicians and committeemen who were admitted to the house to extend their congratulations and tributes. But Woody Hayes was not inside. He was still at the North Facility making his "victory" statement to reporters and posing for pictures. The pictures, which would all show him with his big gap-toothed grin, were being taken less than a day after Hayes, his face drooping and his hand trembling, had said, "We knew we had to win to go and we didn't." In twenty-four hours it had all changed. But then again, it had not.

Sunday night. It is raining heavily now outside the house on Cardiff. The crowd has long since dispersed, and some paper streamers strung through a few trees are the only remaining signs of the afternoon celebration. Inside the house the telephone is ringing repeatedly with shrill felicitations. Though the phone is close at hand, Woody Hayes ignores it. Coach Hayes is not available tonight. The phone echoes through the house, falls silent for a moment, then begins again. In a nearby office Big Ed Weaver and other Ohio State athletic officials are piecing together plans for the trip to Pasadena. Soon the arrangements will be completed: dates, planes, hotel, practice field. Twenty miles to the south, the Hensons, father and son, have something to celebrate. It is still a long shot but maybe with work and a little luck Champ Henson can get his knee back together in time to play in the Rose Bowl.

But Woody Hayes sits alone in his living room tonight, temporarily numb to the world he craves. Despite the smiles for the cameras, he is not happy. His victory has come in the boardroom, not on the football field. The national championship is no more and there is no one to blame but himself.

Outside the rain will hammer down on the flatlands of Columbus through the night. Mixed emotions in Mudville.

Even one bad day recruiting can kill you later.

The door of the white house on Cardiff Road swings open at 7 A.M. Moments later the pickup with its green Astroturf pulls away from the curb and lumbers out toward the interstate.

For Woody Hayes and his Ohio State football machine, it is just another ordinary workday. Nothing special at all, even though today, February 14, 1974, is Coach Hayes's sixty-first birthday.

Considering Hayes's power and influence at Ohio State and in Columbus, his birthday should be a glorious social event for the school and the city. But there has never been an official celebration and probably never will be. Winning football games does have its price. And that the man who must keep the Machine going cannot let up for a minute, even on his birthday, shows just how high that price can be. February 14 falls in the middle of the recruiting season, and Coach Hayes does not have time for such frivolities as birthday parties. As he often points out, "Even one bad day recruiting can kill you later." So on his birthday, Wayne Woodrow Hayes, now sixty-one years old, has to be out on the interstate at 7 A.M., heading toward Dayton in search of seventeen-year-old boys.

Working on holidays is nothing new. He has always treated Christmas, the Fourth of July and Thanksgiving like any other day. Purdue coach Alex Agase tells of the Ohio prospect he thought he had persuaded to come to his school, then Northwestern. Thanksgiving Day Agase phoned the youngster at home to wish him a happy holiday, only to learn that Hayes was in the kitchen helping carve the turkey. Agase's prospect ended up at Ohio State. "Every time I tell that one at a banquet in front of Woody," says Agase, "he just leans back and roars."

On his sixty-first birthday his assistant coaches are out working, too, each one on the road recruiting and speculating perhaps on whether any of them will ever stand in his place. "I'd bet the house and car that Woody will never retire," says one of his aides. "He couldn't live without football. If he got out he'd go crazy. He's not the type to quietly live out his final years playing golf or fishing. He's still a driven, dedicated man. They're going to have to carry him off the football field when the time comes."

When the time comes. But for now, as he drives his pickup down Interstate 70, Woody Hayes appears to be in good health. He doesn't drink or smoke, and on his sixty-first birthday, despite his weight, his heart seems strong. Surprisingly, he has never had an ulcer. Three of his quarterbacks —Cornelius Greene, Rex Kern and Tom Matte—and several assistants have had them, but he never has. He's just a carrier.

If he weren't so preoccupied today with thoughts of recruiting and future teams, he might sit back in his pickup and review the accomplishments and good fortune of his life and career. His wife, Anne, a genuine football widow, had always been understanding, cheerful and supportive. His twenty-eight-year-old son, Steven, had just married, was following a law career in the county prosecutor's office and perhaps with his father's assistance might one day enter politics.

Hayes had worked fiendishly hard all those years, but never for money. Money still meant nothing to him. Other famous coaches who had climbed to the top had earned thousands through product endorsements and business investments. Nobody was surprised when Alabama's Bear Bryant, coaching's answer to J. Paul Getty, gave one hundred thousand dollars in stocks to his university. But Hayes had never made a penny, aside from his relatively low coaching salary and minor outside earnings, and at sixty-one he was neither broke nor wealthy. Along with the modest house on Cardiff, all he owned were forty-five acres in the hills of southeastern Ohio, and because the land was stripmined, it had been bought at the bargain-basement rate of fifteen dollars an acre. He rarely found time to go there, but if he ever got around to it, he told friends, he would build a log cabin and try to reclaim the flayed ground. There was a rumor he would cover it with Astroturf.

He had outlived almost all his old friends. Lombardi,

whom he used to call "Coach Vince," was one of them. The two men had hit it off immediately when they first met in the mid-Fifties. Maybe it was because the similarities between them were so striking, from their gapped front teeth and big paunches to their philosophies on and off the field. Lombardi was fond of Hayes because he, more than any other coach in America, mirrored Lombardi's social and football beliefs. Like Hayes, Lombardi thought most social problems—as well as disciplinary troubles on his team—should be solved by cracking down as hard as possible on the offenders. Like Hayes, he clashed often with reporters, had an explosive temper and played every game to the brim of his ego. Judged from Lombardi's viewpoint—that winning was the only thing—Hayes was not only the best coach in football but also an almost-perfect man, a symbol of all that was brave and good in American life.

It wasn't surprising, then, that Hayes, after Lombardi's death in 1970, seemed to step into the vacant spot in the starting lineup of Middle America's main men. Though only a football coach, Lombardi had grown into a national figure, a man who inspired strong emotions, stirred the extremes of worship and hate, and nobody could deny that Hayes was marching to a similar drummer. In the Watergate era, he was one of the few conservative heroes still winning.

Beyond that, he was still the master of his Machine. At an age when many men dreamed of Florida condominiums, Hayes was working harder than ever. To him, it wasn't a question anymore of proving himself. He had already done that. He was the oldest active college coach in the country now and only one other, Bear Bryant, had won more games. Even if it ended today, only two other coaches, Frank Leahy of Notre Dame and Bernie Bierman of Minnesota, would have won more national championships. At this point it was a question of winning more. He couldn't stop now even if he wanted to.

Despite numerous offers from professional teams, who had actually expected him to jump at the chance, he had remained at Ohio State. From time to time there were still reports that he might come to the NFL as a coach. But in Columbus, the reports were always laughed at. Most people knew that he preferred commanding his own football organization to taking orders from any owner or general manager. Besides, he has explained, "Those pro players might try to kill me."

His own players and even his own coaches had been ready to mutiny after the disastrous Michigan game. For a time Hayes found himself facing one of the few serious uprisings of his reign.

The athletic directors' vote to send Ohio State to the Rose Bowl did little to buoy spirits or assuage frustrations in the Buckeye ranks. The day after the decision, the assistant coaches met and voted *not* to go. They were bitterly disappointed by the plodding, stubborn way the Michigan game had been played and angry that their play-calling had been so continually overruled. Their sense of betrayal was heightened by the fact that they had been so loyal and had prepared so long, each putting in almost as many hours as Coach Hayes himself. And they did not relish the idea of returning to Pasadena, where the team had lost two Rose Bowl games in a row, for more of the same.

Hayes had to act fast and he knew it. If word of the coaches' vote leaked out to his players, who were also bitching about the Michigan fiasco, he would almost certainly have a full-scale rebellion on his hands. He needed time to breathe. Without committing himself, he listened to the assistants and promised to consider a more varied attack in California. Though finding himself on the defensive, a situation which usually drives him into a fury, he remained calm and controlled. Next time, he said, things would be different. He just might rely more heavily on their judgments. "His whole attitude," one assistant remembers, "seemed to be, 'You fellas may have a point there.'"

By talking his way out of it, Hayes got what he was after —a few concessions. The coaches agreed to shelve their vote and leave the question up to the players. Since the players might be swayed if they learned what the coaches had done, Hayes wanted to keep it secret. Many of the players never found out about their coaches' vote.

When the players gathered that afternoon, the North Facility meeting room had an uncharacteristic tension. The atmosphere hardly suited a team that had just gained a Rose Bowl berth. There was no sign of jubilation or excitement. Earlier that day the AP poll had come out, dropping Ohio State to Number 3 in the national rankings, and the disgruntlement was showing itself.

Most of the players had been to Pasadena before and few could say they had found it a congenial place to visit, not with Woody Hayes as tour guide, anyway. For years it had been his practice to take his Buckeyes to the Coast as if they were on some holy crusade. No interviews. No days off. No late nights. No women around. Nothing but tackling and sleeping. "The only fun of being here is winning that game," was the way Woody explained his approach.

But in Ohio State's last two appearances, Hayes and his players had had no fun at all. For all their asceticism, the

Buckeyes had been trounced twice, first by Stanford, 27–17, in 1971, then two years later by USC, 42–17—two teams, ironically, whose coaches favored relaxed training schedules. To most OSU players, the prospect of another Rose Bowl trip was about as alluring as ten days in a Soviet prison camp.

The moment Hayes walked into the room, the rows of stony faces told him the story: The players were of the same mind as their coaches. "He started out acting friendly and smiling a lot," one player recalls. "He never really apologized or took the blame for the Michigan game. But he promised that next time out in Pasadena everything would be different. He said we'd do some passing and also there was going to be more freedom and a lot less restrictions. He made a whole bunch of promises. It was like a campaign speech. I'm telling you I've never seen Woody like that. Man, he must've been scared shitless about what we were going to do.

"Then after making all these promises, he says, 'All right, now, how many of you fellas want to go to the Rose Bowl?' And he really glared at us when he said it. About half the dudes raised their hands, I think more out of fear than anything else. But the other half, myself included, didn't move. Then he says, 'Now, who *doesn't* want to go?' Well, shit, who the hell is going to raise his hand to that? Whoever did, he'd just say, 'Okay, mister, then you don't go,' and the guy's career would be over. What a way to take a vote. I know this: If there had been a secret ballot, we'd have said to hell with it. But this was democracy, Woody-style."

Regardless of the method, there was no quarreling with the result. For the time being, he was over the hump. But the coaches' vote had told him something. These coaches and players might be willing to pay the Hayes price—the long hours, the bodily punishment, the anguish, the humiliation

—to win. But not to lose. His Machine, now threatened by a disorganized but potentially dangerous group of dissidents, would have to be put right again. However much he might personally abhor appeasement, something would have to be done. If he didn't do something, the team wouldn't stand a chance on New Year's Day. USC, Ohio State's opponent once again, would win easily, and another Rose Bowl loss could seriously damage the Machine. Change, or at least the appearance of it, would have to come.

And so it was a "new" Woody Hayes who stepped off the plane in California ten days before the game. An amazing transformation was underway. Woody Hayes, the grim dictator who had always kept his players under lock and key as if they were wanted for murder, had suddenly become Woody Hayes, the cheerful civil libertarian, letting his players engage in the wildest forms of dissipation. He let them stay out till 2 A.M. He let them practice once instead of twice a day. He let them take whole days off. He let them go to parties. He let them spend New Year's Eve in their hotel, rather than make the traditional trip to a mountain monastery. He let his married players sleep in the same room with their wives. He even let some of his players talk to reporters.

The new image Woody was projecting threw everyone off balance, especially the Rose Bowl press corps, who had become conditioned to his rages. Here was the wicked witch of the Midwest suddenly turned into a walking advertisement for Dale Carnegie, arriving at daily news briefings smiling broadly, bestowing compliments and exuding good will. Each news conference was an exercise in polite dart-dodging and gracious thrust-parrying. Instead of sour displays of temper he gave the reporters poise and aplomb. Instead of clenched fists he gave them avuncular charm. Once he even gave them four of his first-string players to interview. It was enough to send some of the writers, notably Jim Murray of the Los Angeles *Times,* into an acute state of culture shock. "The long-time Woody-watchers," wrote Murray, "couldn't have been more thunderstruck to see William of Orange doing the cha-cha-cha."

Each day of the pregame week brought fresh stories in the West Coast papers of what one writer called Hayes's "personality transplant." His tantrums, once the staple of the holiday-season sports pages, were replaced by reports of his kindly disposition and good deeds: Woody sitting on Santa's knee at the Ohio State Christmas party; Woody winning friends and charming people on the Johnny Carson show; Woody calling off practice to give players extra free time.

His miraculous metamorphosis carried through the game itself on New Year's Day. As promised, he had turned his players loose off the field, and now, as promised, he was turning them loose on it. If USC, which had the best passer in the country in Pat Haden and a half-dozen All-Americans, didn't believe that Ohio State was capable of mounting a modern offense—with faking, option plays and even passes —it soon would. On a chilly, smog-filled afternoon USC would find out the hard way.

For much of the game it looked as if Woody might shed his new persona any minute, as the Trojans ran up 3–0, 14–7 and 21–14 leads, mostly on Haden's footwork and passing. Running, scrambling and throwing with infuriating ease, Haden was singlehandedly putting limp hangdog expressions on the faces of the Buckeye defenders. To make matters worse, Ohio State's new baroque offense suffered an early blow when Cornelius Greene's first pass of the day was badly overthrown and picked off.

It was after USC's third touchdown in the middle of the third quarter that the game seemed to turn around. "Get the hell off the field, you sonofabitch," a furious Hayes shouted at defensive tackle Arnie Jones, who had muffed a fumble recovery. Woody the gentle was suddenly the Woody of old. Summoning the entire defensive unit around him, he erupted into one of his purple-faced, foot-stomping, fist-pounding fits, ranting for a full minute and looking as though he were going to tear the shoulder pads off Randy Gradishar, a major victim of Haden's artistry. Perhaps it was the welcome sight of their coach stepping back into character. Perhaps it would have happened anyway. But for the rest of the afternoon the Buckeye defenders did not give up a single point. They never really stopped the perfect spirals of Haden, who threw 21 completions and engineered 27 first downs, but they managed to wear him down. A tired Haden was able to control the ball but not the game.

With the defense stiffening, and Woody keeping his commitment to new modes of attack, and runners like Archie Griffin and Pete Johnson tearing into USC's middle, and Cornelius Greene actually doing some passing, the Buckeyes laid on 28 points in the final twenty minutes and took charge of the game. It wasn't exactly what the broadcasters would call an aerial circus: Greene put the ball up only 8 times. But it was the quality of his passes. Every throw stung USC except the first, the one intercepted. After that the Ohio State faithful would have bet their Buckeye rings that Woody was going to send the forward pass back to the closet. But this time he had no choice. He had pledged himself to reform. Besides, Greene, deservedly voted player-of-the-game, was running the plays off so fast that Hayes might not have had time to veto them even if he'd wanted to.

Later, after USC had been mutilated 42–21, a beaming Woody Hayes stood on a platform outside the Rose Bowl locker rooms and said, "I don't mind telling you this is the greatest victory I've ever had, the greatest *we've* ever had."

It was more than mere phrase-making or locker-room hyperbole or even politicking to get the lost Number 1 ranking restored. With all the pressures he had been under, from his own organization and from Big Ten officials desperately in need of a win, it was obvious he meant exactly what he said. This was his day to celebrate and throughout it his eyes danced and he laughed exultantly at the lifting of his burdens. He lavished praise on everybody: on his defeated opponents, on his players, on his coaches, on the athletic directors and even on the press. Then, to complete the astonishment of the sportswriters, he declared in tender parting words: "I love you all."

That was the clincher. The reporters decided that what they had been writing all week was right: Hayes wasn't a Neanderthal coach anymore. In their stories the next day, they wrote lengthy obituaries for Woody the Terrible and introduced Uncle Woody, the kindly old man who had truly changed with the times and was offering his team a new kind of leadership. Unaware of the factors that had brought the so-called changes about, they just switched ribbons and typed that, at last, Woody Hayes had relaxed inside, had *mellowed.*

It was a triumph in public relations, but it was also something more. Throughout his stay in California, the press proved to be a great if unwitting political ally of Hayes, who needed something big and dramatic to counter the lingering bad taste of the Michigan game. The new Woody got as much if not more coverage by the news media than the old

Woody ever did, and Hayes used the media for all it was worth. The stories of his mellowing played a critical role in helping him convince his players he was sincere about reform, that he was willing to give up his prerogatives for the sake of improving team morale. That in turn helped prepare his players to put out their best on the field. Such sophisticated forms of public relations had never been necessary before, but this time Woody Hayes was running scared. It was a psychological master stroke.

In a sense, his strategy was airtight. By allowing more freedom on and off the field, measures he personally disliked, Hayes couldn't lose. If Ohio State won, the dissidents would be out of his hair and most likely all would be forgiven and forgotten. If the Buckeyes lost he could argue that the new approach was worse than the old and abandon it without a whimper from anybody.

"The amazing thing about the whole Rose Bowl scene," one Ohio State player pointed out later, "was the way the old man turned everything that was against him to his advantage. Last year he smashed a photographer and all the sportswriters ganged up on him. So this year he comes on all sweetness and light. Not only does he have the reporters eating out of his hand, but he's got them writing propaganda to help his relations with the team.

"Last year we went out to California, got treated like animals and got killed 42–17. We didn't see California, we didn't do anything but practice. When it came time to play nobody gave a shit about anything but getting out. This year was completely different. The married dudes stayed with their wives. Some of the single dudes were copping chicks in their rooms and nobody said a word. There were no disciplinary problems this year because Woody stopped disciplining us. Not because he's grown soft with age or become liberal or mellowed or any of that bullshit, but because he *had* to. Guys were ready to quit.

"It was the same thing with passing. He had no alternatives. He had to let us pass no matter how much he hated the idea. A lot of people talk like Woody never used the forward pass before. People have short memories. Rex Kern passed some and others did, too—but it just never caught on with Woody. You got to remember, this is a dude who refers to a touchdown pass as 'a cheap one.' Can you believe that? What the hell does he mean, 'cheap'? I count six points, doesn't he? And if we'd have lost that game, I guarantee you this, he would have blamed it on our passing. That's right! Our passing and the amount of freedom he gave us.

"I got a kick out of those articles about how he's mellowed. Did you see him out there in the third quarter giving hell to everybody? You wouldn't call that mellowing, now would you? He's not really changed. Next year he'll be back doing things pretty much the same way he's been doing them for twenty-three years. But you've got to give the man credit. He understood the politics of the Rose Bowl situation perfectly. He knew what he had to do and he was usually one step ahead of everybody. I've been telling people for a long time, this is one awesome dude."

Hayes's miracle of modern salesmanship came just in time. With the recruiting season coming up during the next few months, it was essential to get his Machine rolling smoothly again. And he had done it. The Rose Bowl win went a long way toward defusing the threat of revolt. In many ways it emphasized a point Coach Hayes himself frequently makes: "Winning takes care of everything."

The dissenters and pressures to win weren't the only problems facing Woody Hayes during the days in Pasadena. There was also the matter of the special Rose Bowl fund for his assistant coaches.

Three weeks before the trip, several hundred letters had been sent out to members of the Athletic Committee and other big-money supporters, asking for contributions to help defray the assistant coaches' expenses in California. One of the letters landed in the lap of the editor of the *Citizen-Journal* and was brought to the attention of a university official. Suddenly Woody Hayes had a slush-fund scandal on his hands.

Richard Armitage, an Ohio State vice president in charge of overseeing athletic department affairs, was genuinely shocked when he read the letter. The university had always permitted the athletic department to raise money for such things as scholarships and new facilities, but never for the pockets of staff members. It was one thing for an assistant coach to make a few extra bucks by fudging on his recruiting expenses, but this was a case of Ohio State employees hustling bonuses through the mail, and on university stationery yet.

No one had said anything before about the coaches' needing expense money beyond what they always got for the Rose Bowl. The coaches made between fourteen and eighteen thousand dollars a year, plus healthy expense allowances, and if provisions were inadequate, Armitage wanted to know, why hadn't they simply come to the university? Armitage quickly ordered the fund drive stopped, directing that the money collected so far—about seven thousand dollars—be put into the athletic scholarship fund or returned.

At first Hayes tried to minimize the impact of the fund

controversy, blaming it all on a misunderstanding brought about by faulty communications. But he was deeply shaken, partly from fear of a reprise of 1956, when he had been placed on probation for handing out money to players. His next approach was to look innocent and say he had nothing at all to do with the fund. The only flaw in that strategy was that the letters had been signed "Your grateful friend, Woody." And there was no way he could avoid the reality of what the letters said: that he himself planned to contribute a thousand dollars to help the assistants and their families meet "incidental expenses in the way of clothing, entertainment and other various things."

By the time Hayes got back to Columbus the headlines were coming up on page one. It was reported that the fund was nothing new, that similar collections had been made for both of the team's two previous trips to Pasadena. The papers weren't mincing words, either, dubbing it the "Rose Bowl slush fund." The interest of IRS officials was also awakened by one part of the letter claiming contributions would be tax deductible. An IRS official was quoted as saying that serious tax problems could be involved, not only with the fund, which lacked tax-exempt status, but also for the recipients of the money. He promised an investigation that might include looking into the coaches' tax returns. Meanwhile true to form, Ohio State athletic director Big Ed Weaver was making things look worse than they actually were, at first denying any knowledge of the fund, then later admitting he had approved it.

To help clear the air, Armitage suggested bringing the case before the university's Athletic Council, an eleven-man body of faculty, alumni and students, responsible, in theory, for keeping an eye on the athletic department. That was the best way, Armitage said, to determine whether the coaches had done wrong and to set policy for the future. That was also the best way of assuring that the controversy would be swept cleanly under the rug.

The council was not known for brazen defiance of Woody Hayes and his football program. It was, in effect, *his* council, and in its nineteen years of existence, had rarely challenged him on the budgets and policies it was supposed to scrutinize. In general its members were happy to do what Hayes expected of them.

So not many people were astonished when, two months after hearing testimony on the slush fund, the council finally drew up recommendations that were so vague that the two newspapers in town printed differing versions of what they meant. Beneath a welter of officialese, the council seemed to be saying that the assistant coaches could, under certain conditions, receive and solicit extra compensation, provided they got the go-ahead from the council first. No one had to be reminded that the council's imprimatur had never been hard to obtain in the past.

Beyond the murky resolutions, no additional steps were taken. A firm policy against fund-raising for the coaches' personal use might have offended the wealthy boosters who supported football and, worse, angered Woody Hayes. That was the last thing the council wanted to do.

The slush fund that had started all the trouble was never mentioned. The resolutions contained not a single word on whether the collections had been proper or would be for future Rose Bowl trips. Thus the council dodged the central issue of the coaches' conduct. As for the money that had been contributed, no one seemed to know where it was or how much, if any, the coaches had returned. When reporters asked what had happened to the money, athletic director Weaver shrugged and said he didn't know. Armitage, however, pronounced himself satisfied that at least the coaches no longer had the money and that none of it had gone to players. His source of information? Big Ed Weaver.

The slush-fund furor lasted many weeks after the Rose Bowl game, but Hayes wasn't perturbed. With the matter safely in the hands of his athletic council, the question was as good as resolved. It was like so many of the problems that had arisen during his long rule. He had always found a way to overcome them. He would survive the slush fund, just as he had survived those post-Michigan days of discontent, just as he had survived the 1956 suspension, just as he had survived the 1961 faculty council uprising, just as he had survived 1966, when the Buckeyes had suffered through that rarity, a losing season, and a small plane was seen circling over Ohio Stadium tugging a huge banner which said, GOODBYE WOODY. He had survived everything.

The internal revolt that had threatened him was, for the moment, dormant. Loosening his iron grip on the organization had been painful, but it had to be done to fix the Machine. Maybe next season, if all went well, he could tighten his grip again.

No doubt about it, 1974 looked like a glorious year. With sixteen of twenty-two regulars returning, including such talent as Griffin and Greene, Colzie and Cusick, the Buckeyes could be expected to finish at or, at worst, near the top once again. Unlike the miserable last month of 1973, things were no longer closing in around him. He had avenged the Rose Bowl losses and taken Wayne Duke and the Big Ten athletic directors off the hook. Schembechler and his Michigan supporters, who were still crying foul, could sputter all they wanted about low-down politicking administrators. If Hayes had his way Schembechler would spend every New Year's Day as he had the last one—watching the games on television and brooding. He had pulled it off. His Buckeyes had been chosen and had come through, which meant that scores of top recruits, viewing the victory on TV, would want to come to Columbus to be winners, too.

That was why he had never felt better, flying home on the Rose Bowl Special to be welcomed by a delirious crowd of five thousand at Port Columbus Airport. It had been exactly one year ago to the day that he had come home a lopsided loser with an assault charge hanging over him. In one year he had turned it all around and was even more powerful. It was an illustration of what enterprise and long hours could bring about. Not to mention a little overnight mellowing.

With the Rose Bowl win behind him, Woody Hayes returned the next day to the task of winning future Rose Bowls, of reinforcing the strength of his Machine by plotting the recruitment of the best high school football players in America.

Recruiting was, above all, what separated the powerful from the powerless, the Ohio States, the USCs and the Oklahomas from the Iowas, the South Carolinas and the Oregons. By running massive recruiting campaigns the incumbent fat cats could control the rise of any potential competition. It was no accident that for years the same small cluster of familiar names had monopolized college football's top ten and the financial rewards of that status. The better players these schools attracted, the stronger and richer they became. And the stronger and richer they became, the better the players they attracted. The result was that one-sided, non-

236

competitive games had more and more become the rule. A kind of Darwinism had set in. Unable to keep up, at least forty-five colleges had dropped varsity football in the last decade and many more were wondering how much longer they could survive. These danger signals had a growing number of people connected with the game calling for changes that would scale down such items as recruiting and bring the many into closer balance with the few.

To Woody Hayes such proposals came from jealous people who didn't understand how things worked. It was only logical that winners, not losers, should receive the rewards. One of the troubles with pro football was that in its zeal to maintain competition, the NFL awarded its worst teams the best draft choices. Society was the same way. People who didn't work got welfare. Everywhere a man looked, except college football, losing and losers were being rewarded. If tight recruiting restrictions became a reality, the weak teams might someday rise up and knock off Ohio State, the Buckeye fans might become restless and stop coming to games, and the Machine would cave in. It was politically wise, then, to keep the weak teams where they were. No, he would never willingly share success, because then it wouldn't be success.

The pickup leaves the interstate and enters the downtown section of Dayton, stopping in front of Patterson Co-op, a racially mixed vocational high school. It is a little after eight o'clock and classes have already started when he gets out and enters the school. He strides briskly into the principal's office and the eyes of the secretaries spring open. His arrival is a big event. They know who he is and why he is here. The principal knows, too, and rushes out to welcome him. He smiles and the principal smiles back gratefully.

It's not far to where he wants to go, but the principal insists on escorting him, moving ahead to hold open the door. Heads turn as he rounds a corner and walks down a long corridor, coming to a halt outside a classroom and waiting while the principal disappears inside. He is completely at home in high schools and can get what he wants without acting pushy. Since he started in coaching he's been inside thousands of them.

The classroom door opens and a neatly dressed young black man steps out. The young man's name is Chris Ward, and he is one of the top senior prospects of 1974. There aren't many young men who stand 6′4″, weigh 275 pounds and can run 40 yards in 4.9 seconds, but Chris Ward is that tall, that heavy, that fast. Chris Ward is what Coach Hayes calls "a quality kid."

He spots Chris Ward and calls out his name. He has seen him four times in the last month—three visits to the high school and one at home—and has often spoken to him by telephone, yet he greets him like a long-lost relative, rushing over and giving him a vigorous two-handed handshake. It's not the best time to talk. Chris Ward is taking a final exam in a civics course. But this won't take long.

"I just dropped by to find out where we stand, son," Woody Hayes says. Behind them the principal, still smiling, heads back to his office.

"I'm still deciding, sir," Chris Ward says.

"All I want to know, son, is Ohio State still in the running?"

"Oh yeah, for sure. I've got it down to three places—Ohio State, Michigan and Indiana."

"All right, now, if I asked you to rate it on a scale of a hundred, where does Ohio stand?"

238

"About sixty-forty for going, sir."

"Umm-hm, not bad," says Woody Hayes, nodding his head. "Umm-hm, not bad at all. You know, son, you could be a great one for us. You look like a football player. You're clean-cut and you're a leader. I could tell the kind of kid you were from meeting your mom and dad. You can always tell by the home, and you come from a dandy one."

"Thank you very much," says Chris Ward.

"You know John Hicks is leaving us," Hayes says, moving closer, "and we need somebody *badly* to fill his big shoes."

"Yes, no doubt about it, he's one of the greats."

"Let me tell you something, son. You remind me of John Hicks. That's right. You could probably step in there and help us out this season."

"Thank you, sir, I'd sure try."

"Yes, you could, son." Woody Hayes's face is only inches from Chris Ward's. "Yes, you could. You know something, son? I have a strong feeling about you. I may be wrong as hell about this, but I think you're gonna come with us at Ohio State. Yes sir, I'd just about bet on it." He is looking Chris Ward in the eye as if trying to stare him down. *"You're gonna be a Buckeye!"*

Another two-handed handshake and Woody Hayes is back on the road again. He must keep moving. By 9 A.M. he is due at another school, this one in Cincinnati, to tell another young man how well he, too, would fit in at Ohio State. There's never a minute to spare. Even on a man's sixty-first birthday, there is so much to do, so many miles to drive, so many young men to talk to.

No one could say how much longer he would go on. Some said he would have to slow down or even step down when, several months after his birthday, he suffered a mild heart attack. But they didn't understand him and they didn't understand the Buckeye spirit. He would be back next season, and, for all anyone knew, at the age of eighty, he might still be there. Still prowling the sideline in that great gray sow of a stadium. Still breathing fire when players missed assignments. Still quoting Emerson and Patton and applying their words to football. Still living with a blackboard and a film projector. Still outworking everybody. Still an original—one of a kind, unmellow, resilient, insatiable, indestructible—and still on top of the college football world.

The buckeye, as the people of Ohio well know, is more than a bitter nut to chew. It's a tough nut to crack.

About the Author

Robert Vare, twenty-nine, is a native New Yorker who received his bachelor's degree in 1967 and, in 1968, his master's degree in classical Greek history from the University of Chicago. He was a reporter for the New York *Post* for three years, and has contributed to many national publications, including *Esquire, The New Republic,* the *Village Voice, Sports Illustrated* and the New York *Times.* Now at work on a novel, he is married and living in Manhattan.